THIS BOOK BELONGS TO

_____

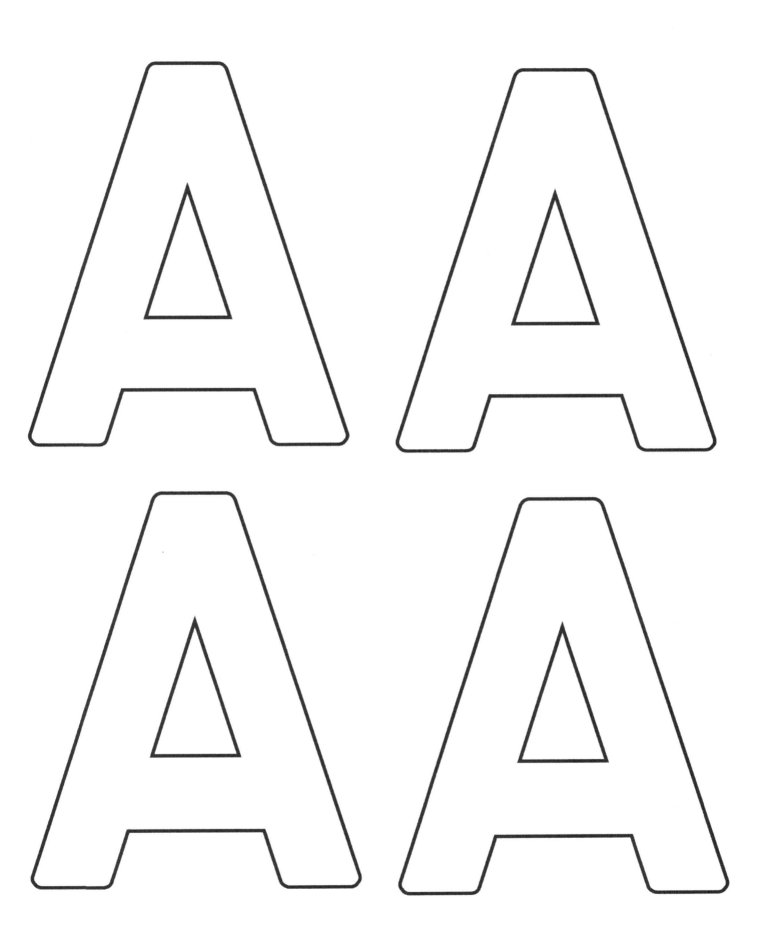

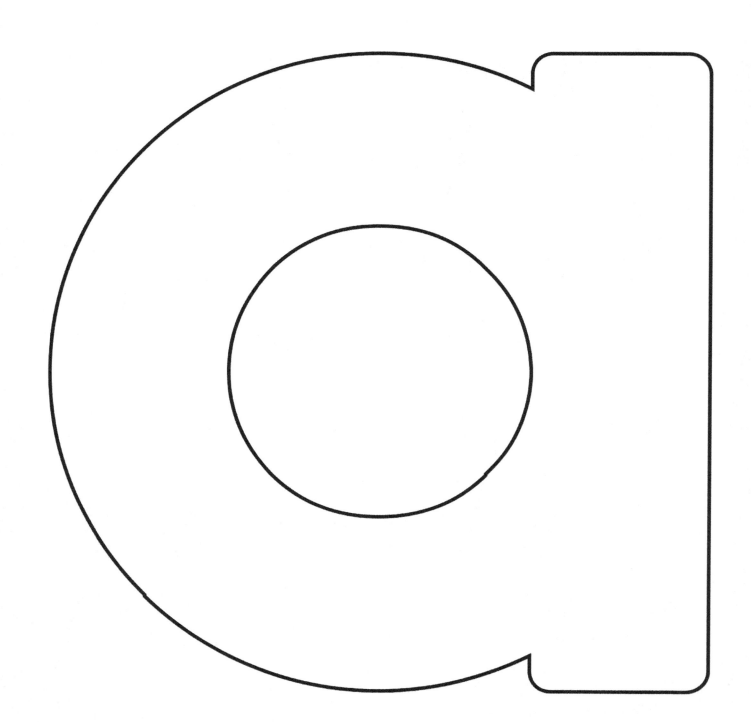

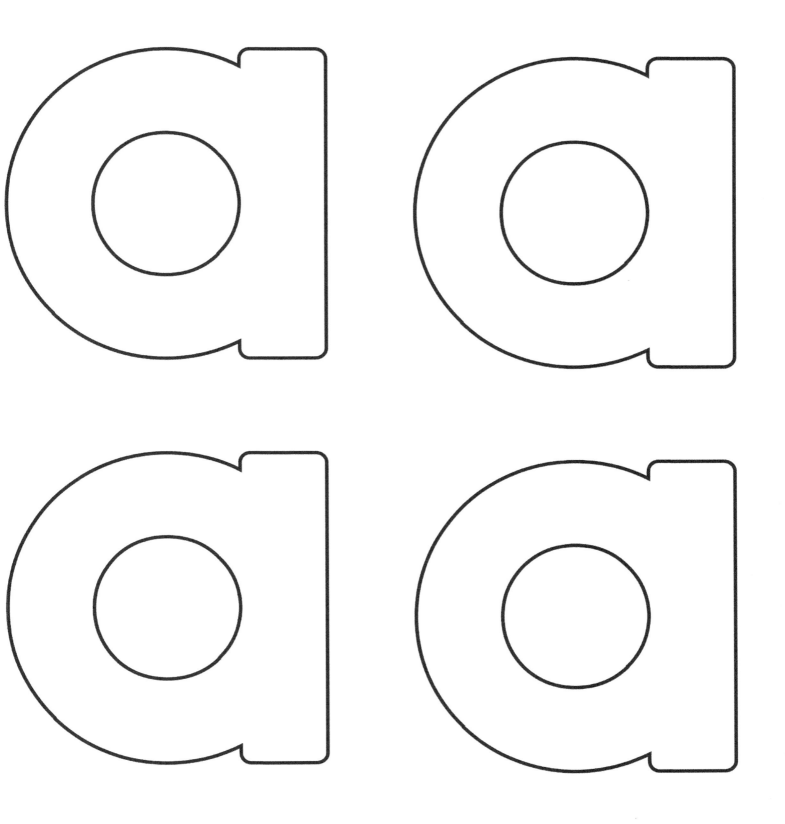

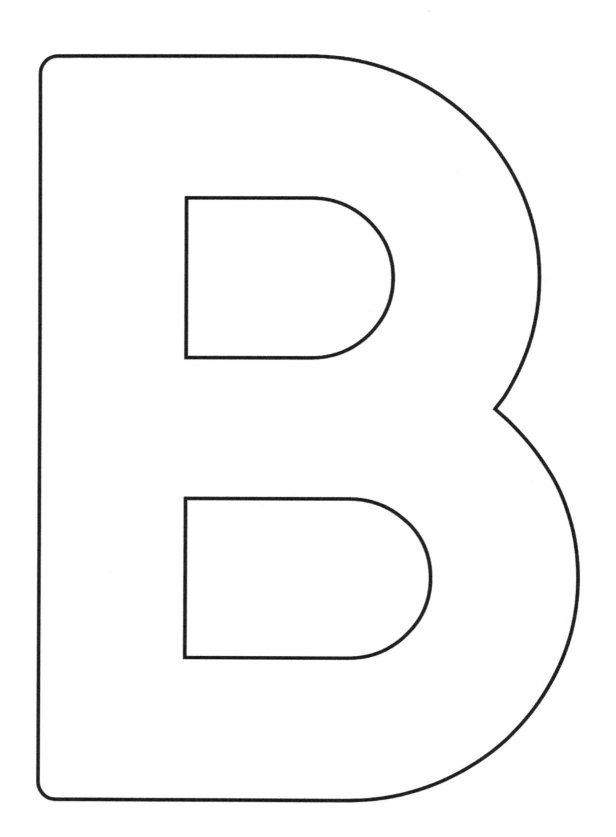

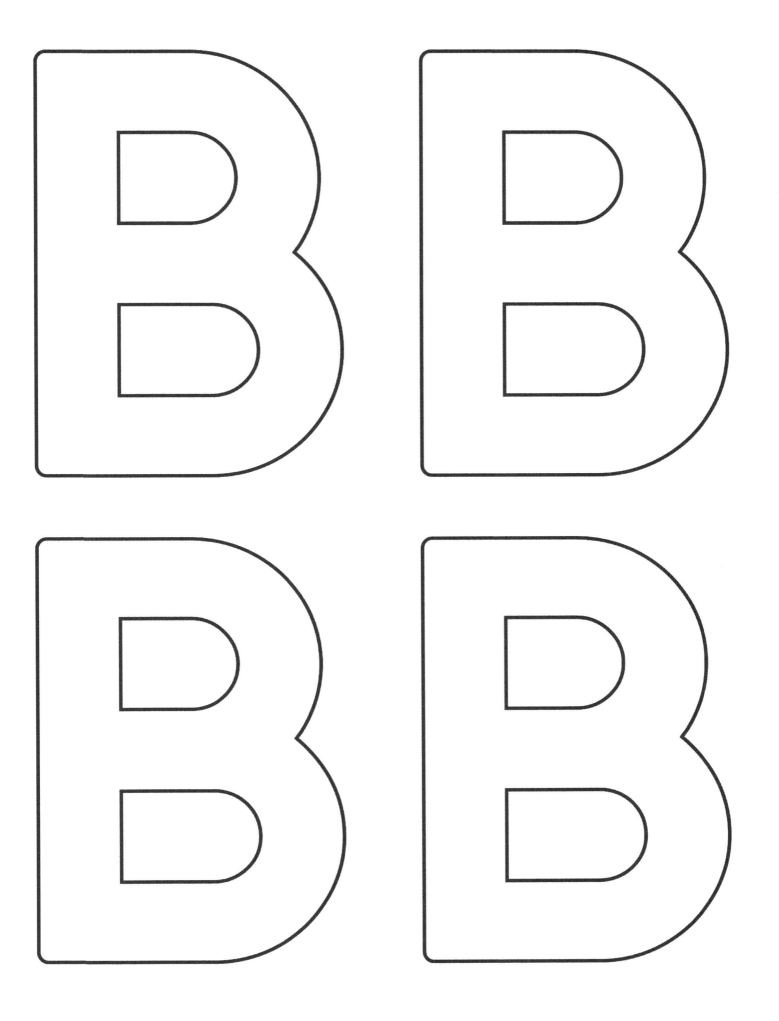

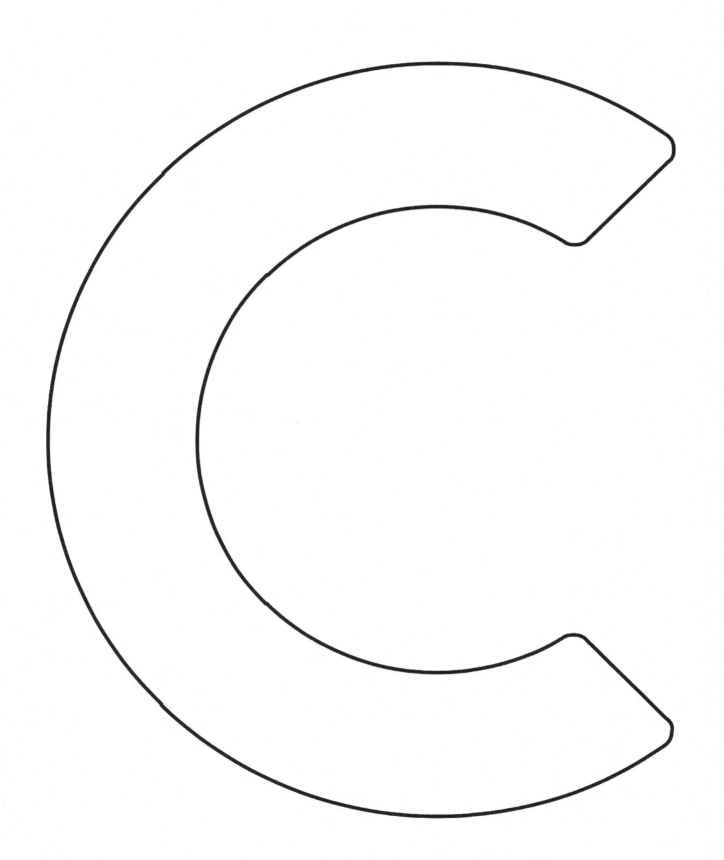

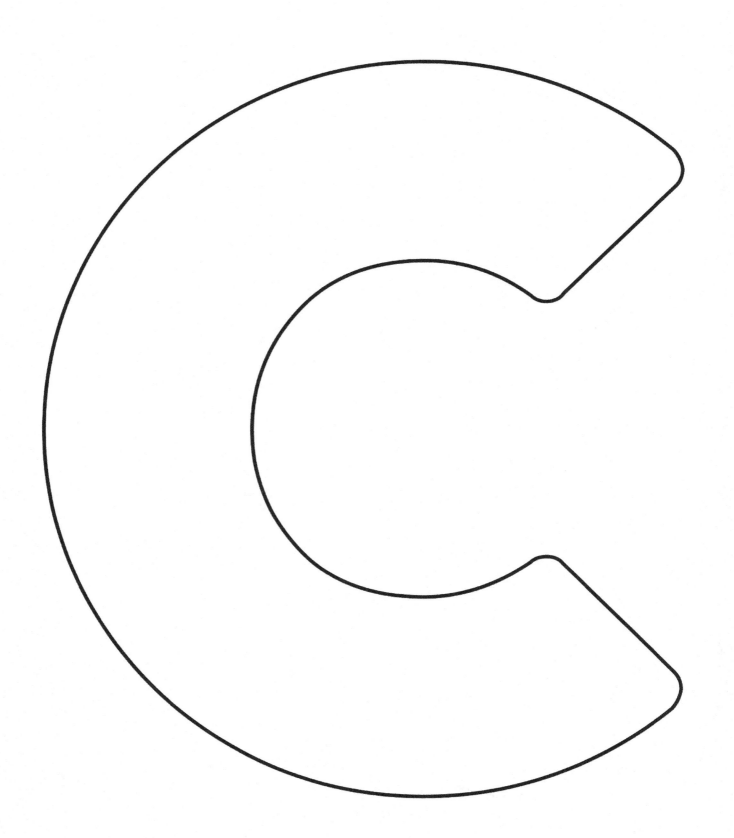

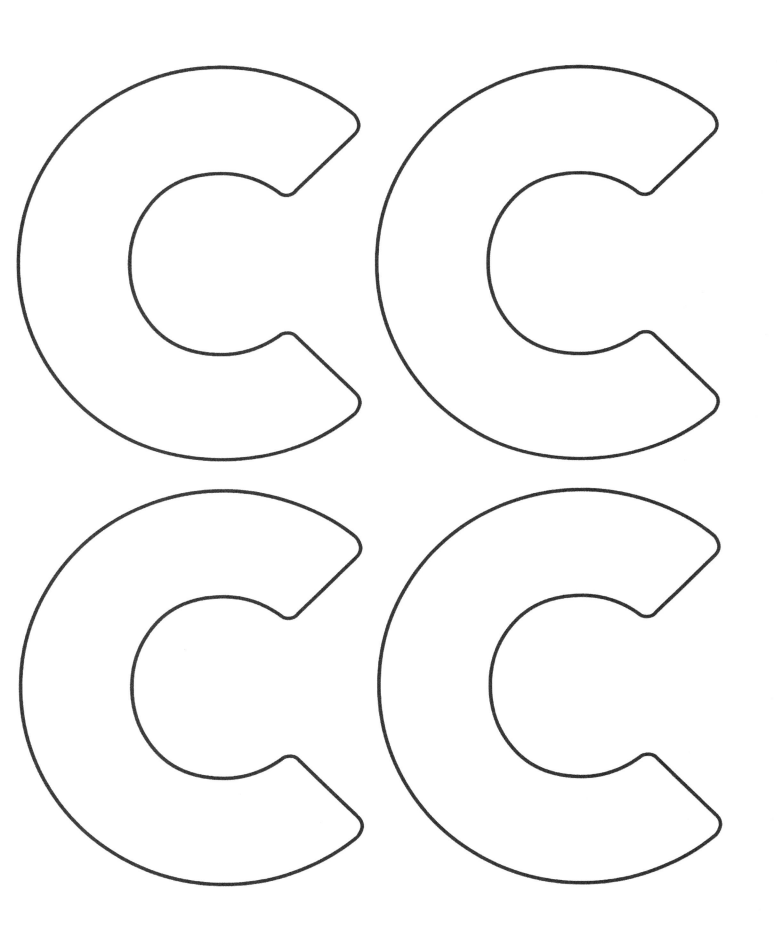

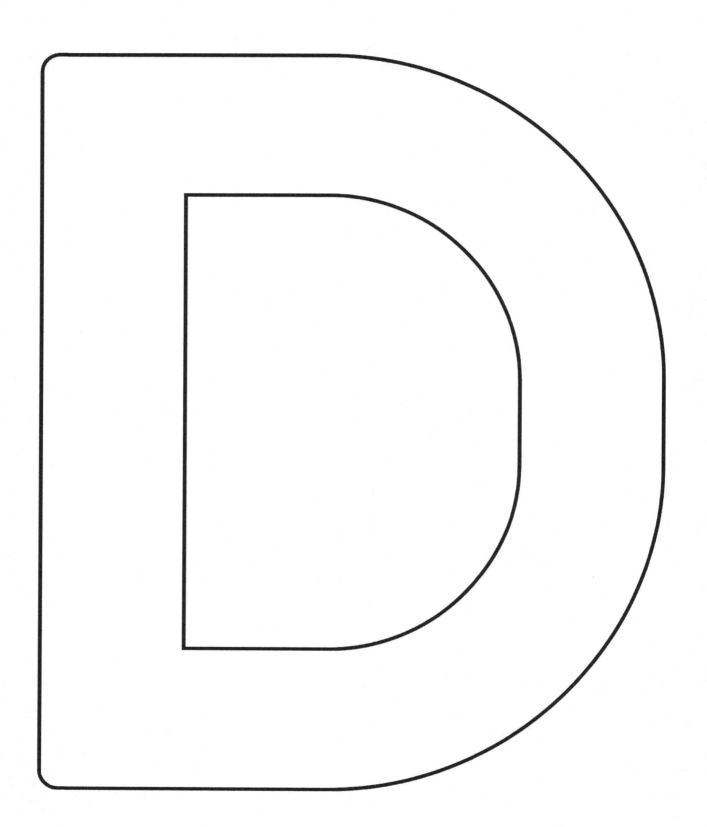

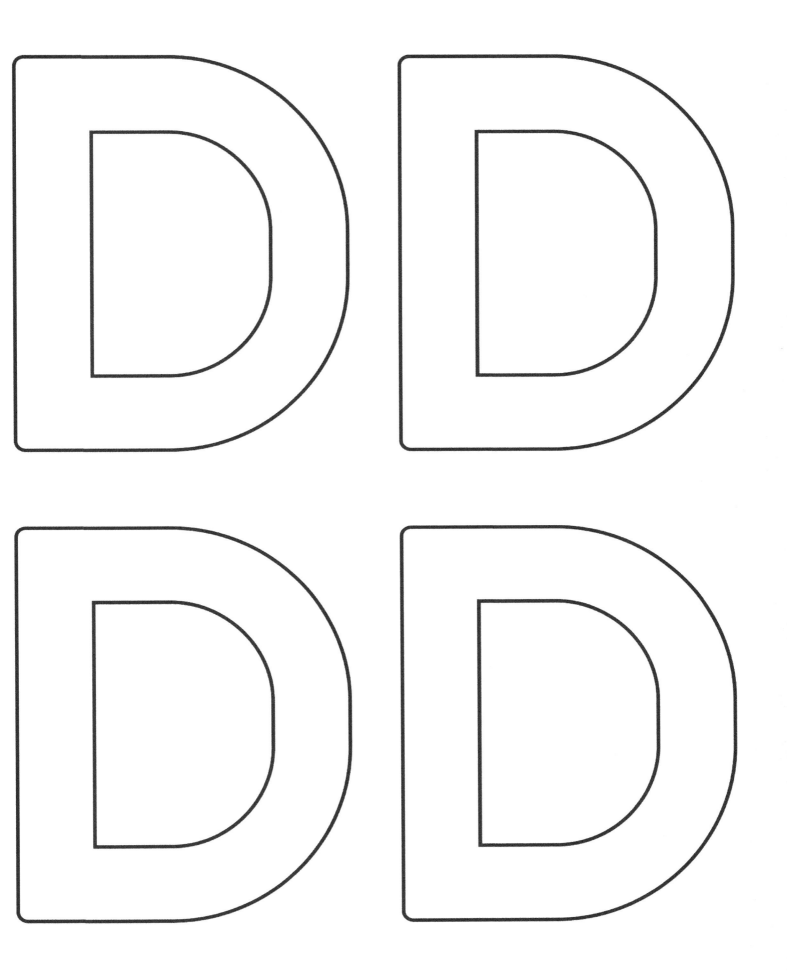

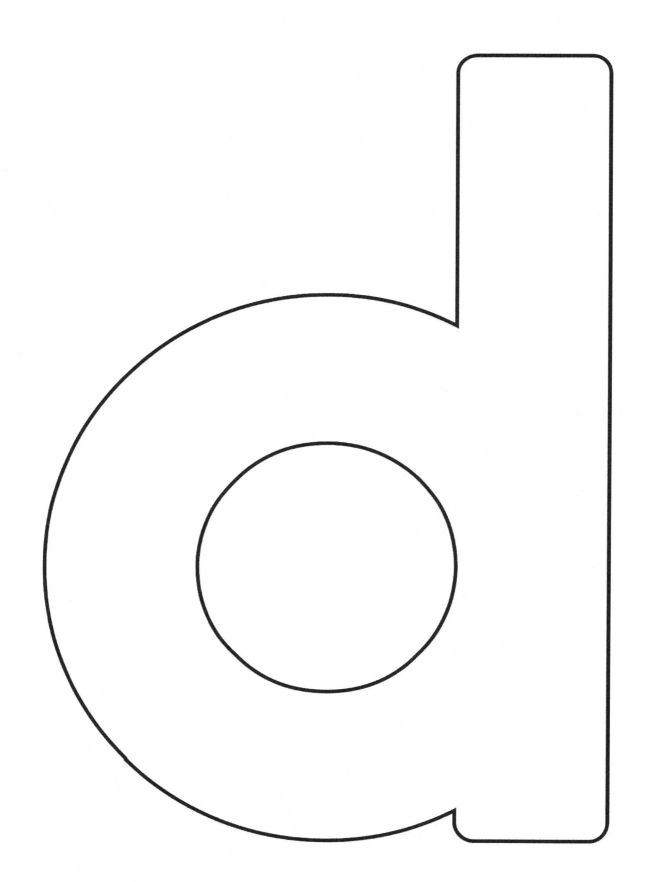

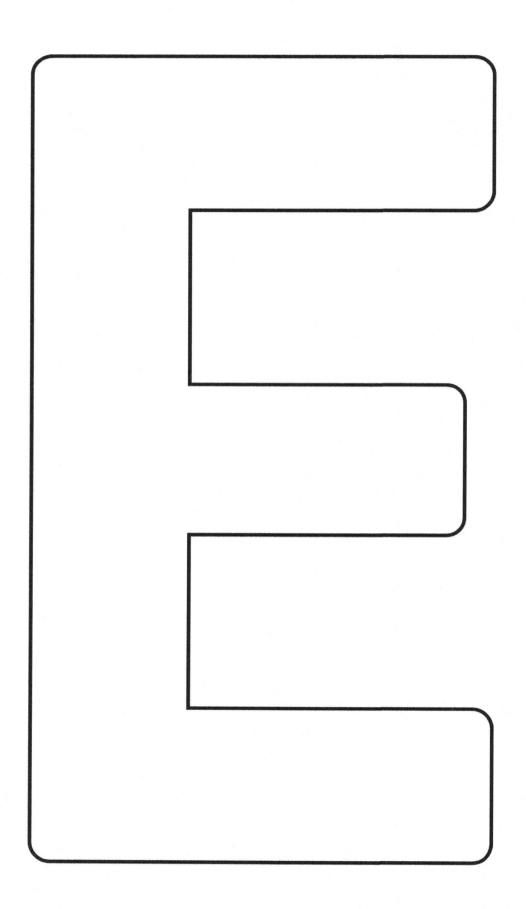

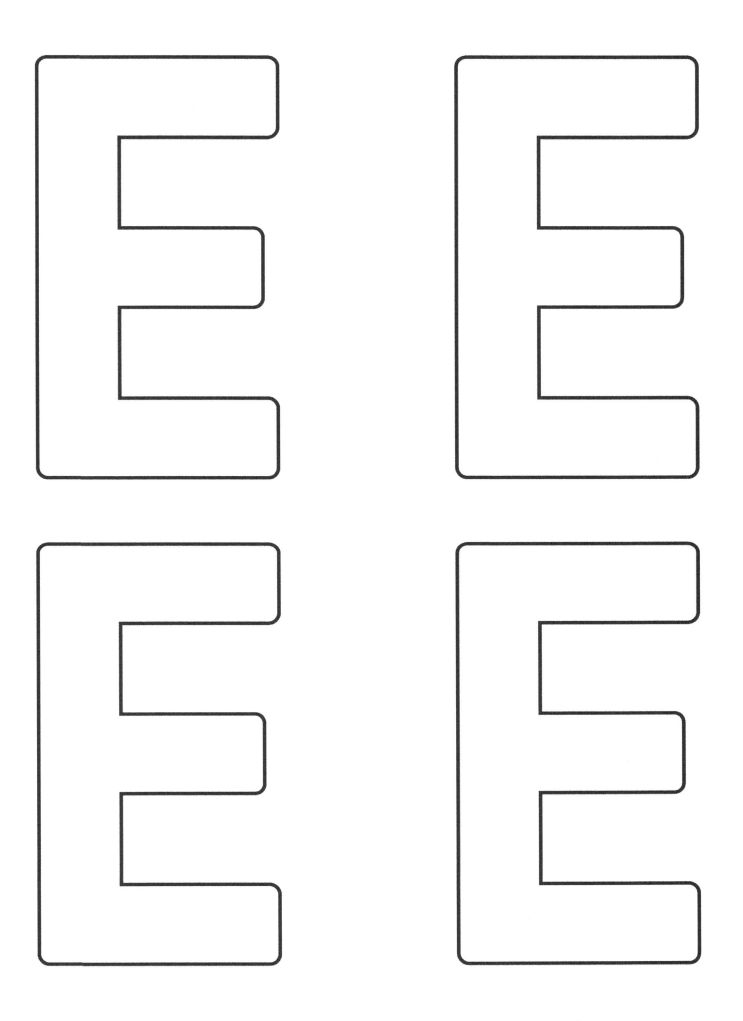

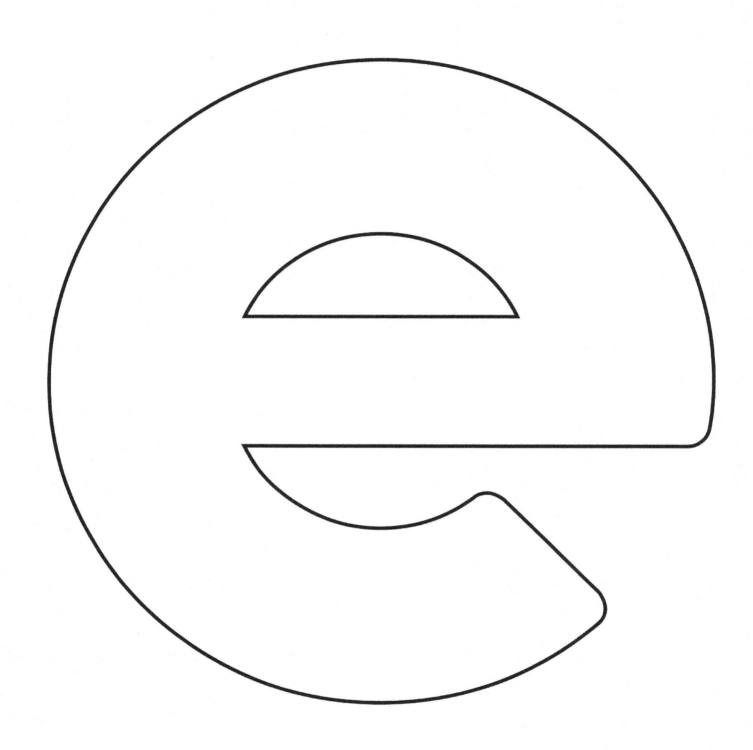

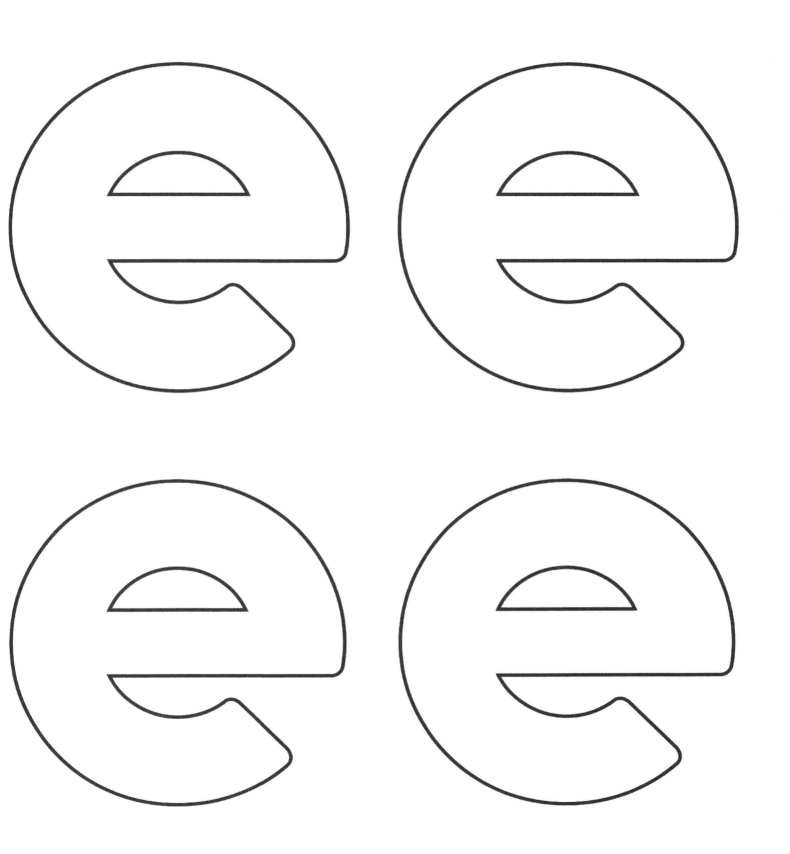

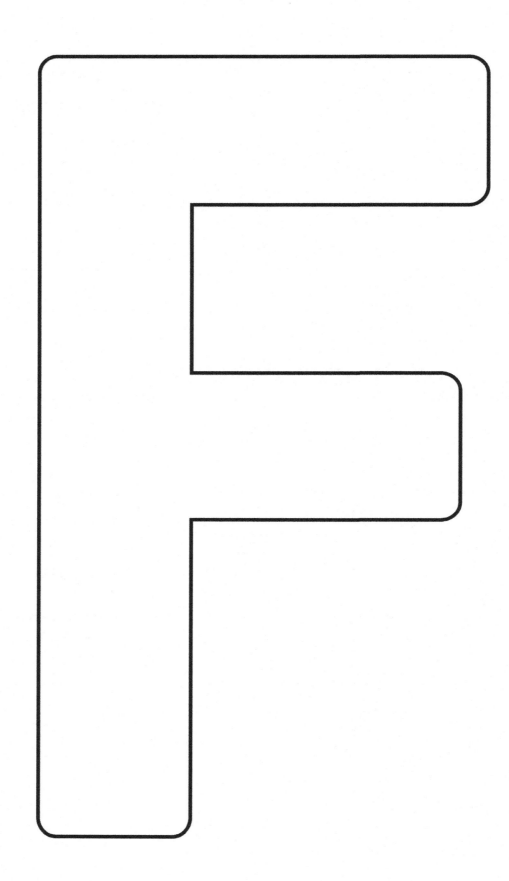

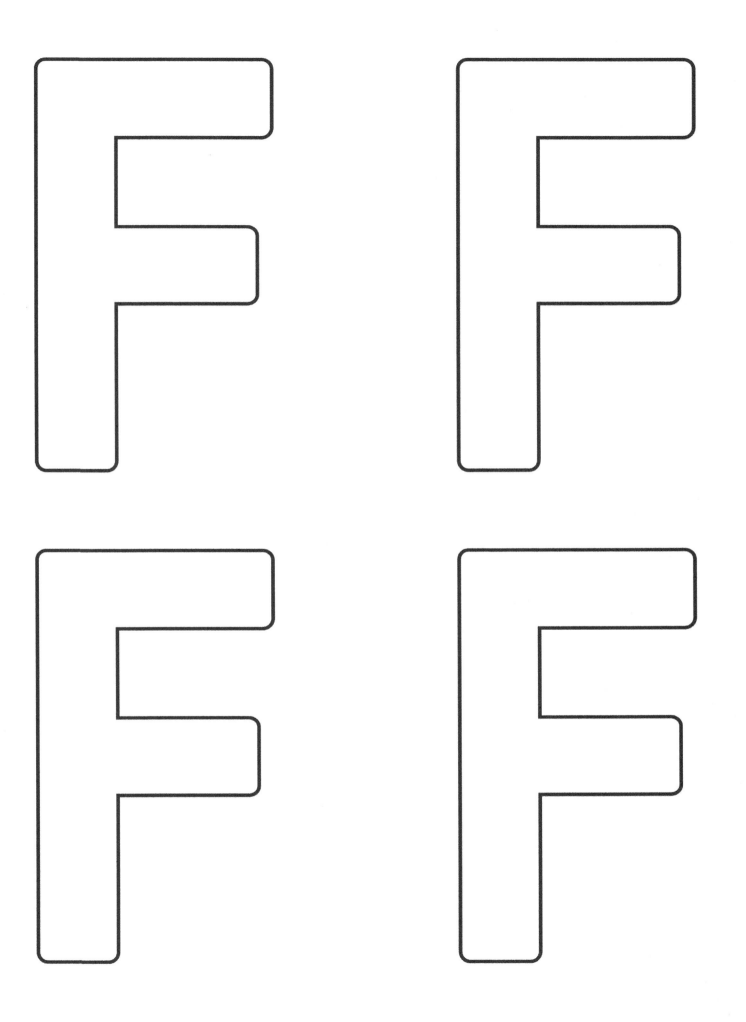

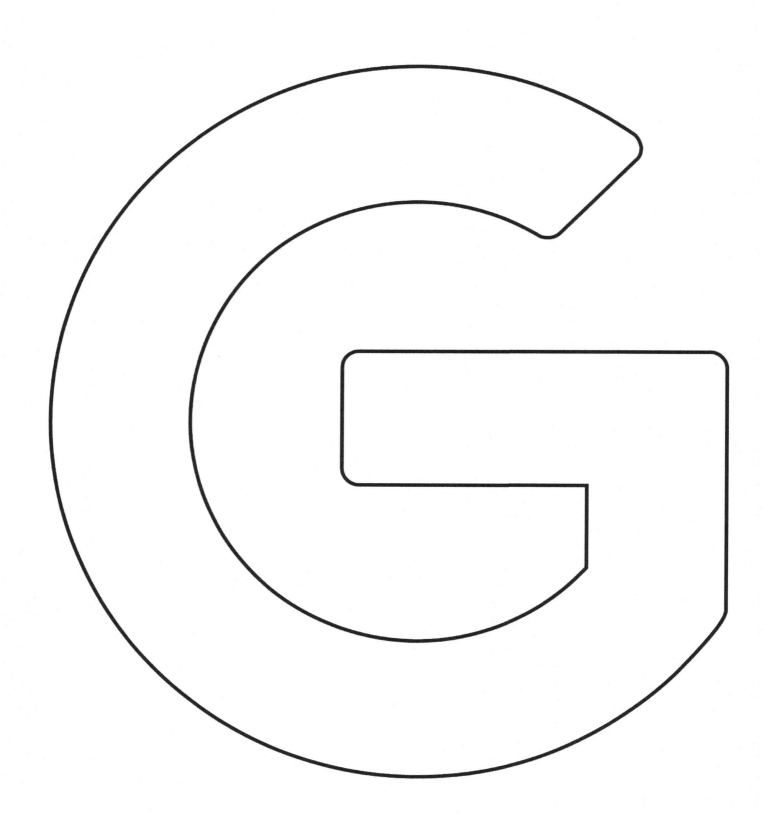

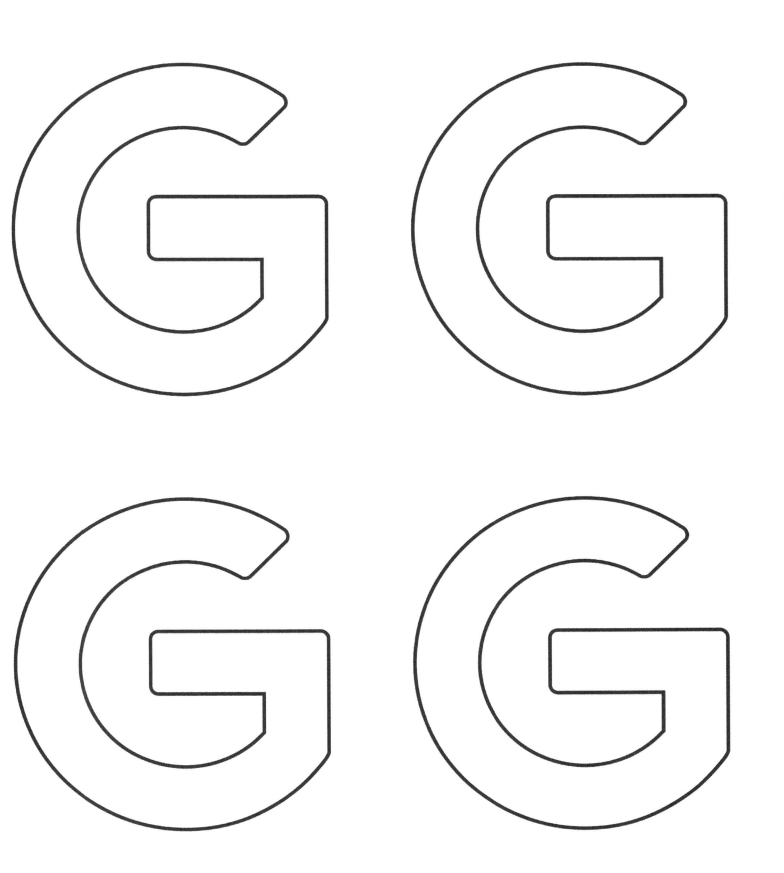

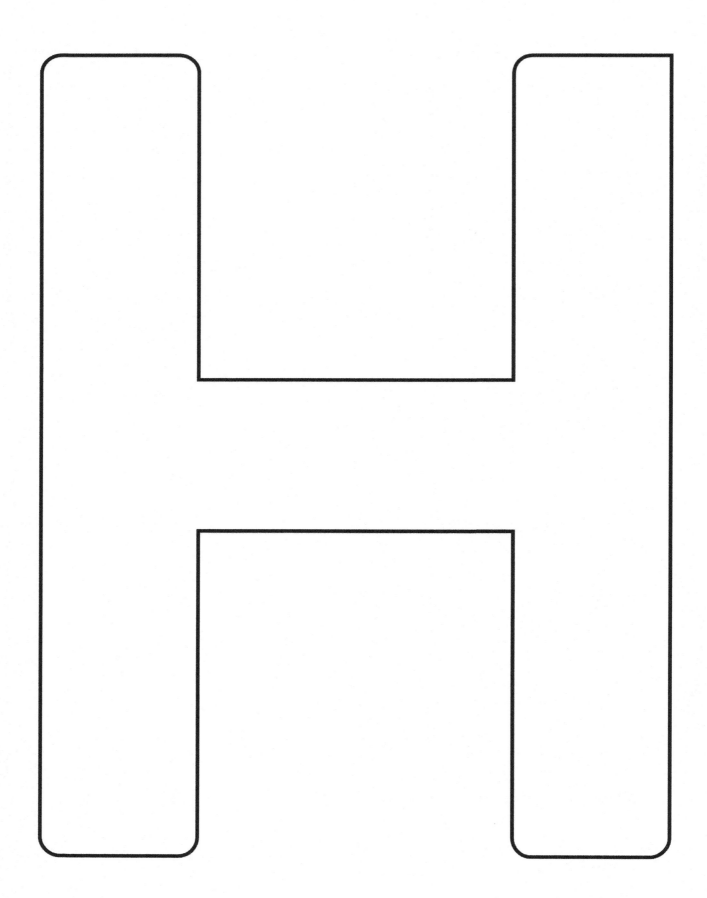

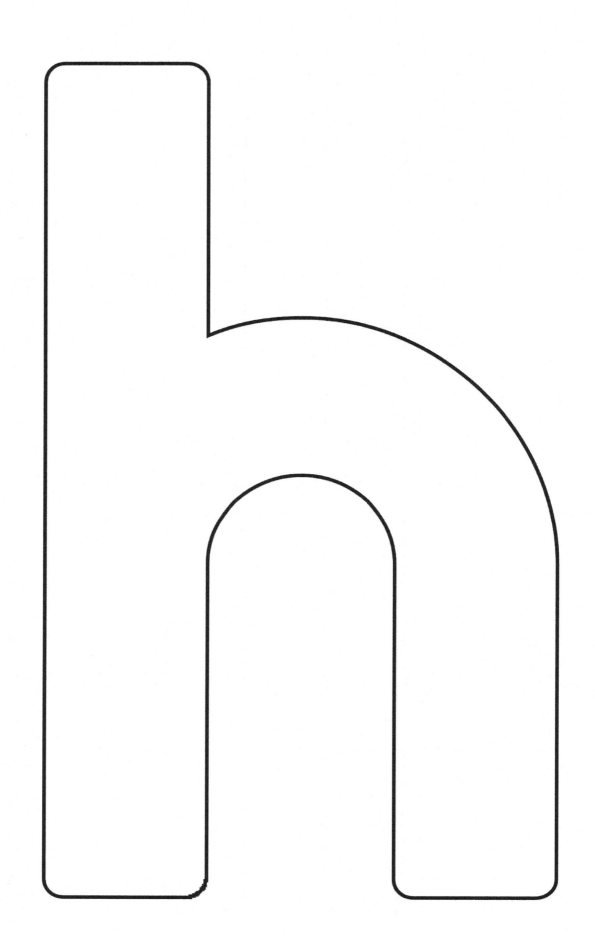

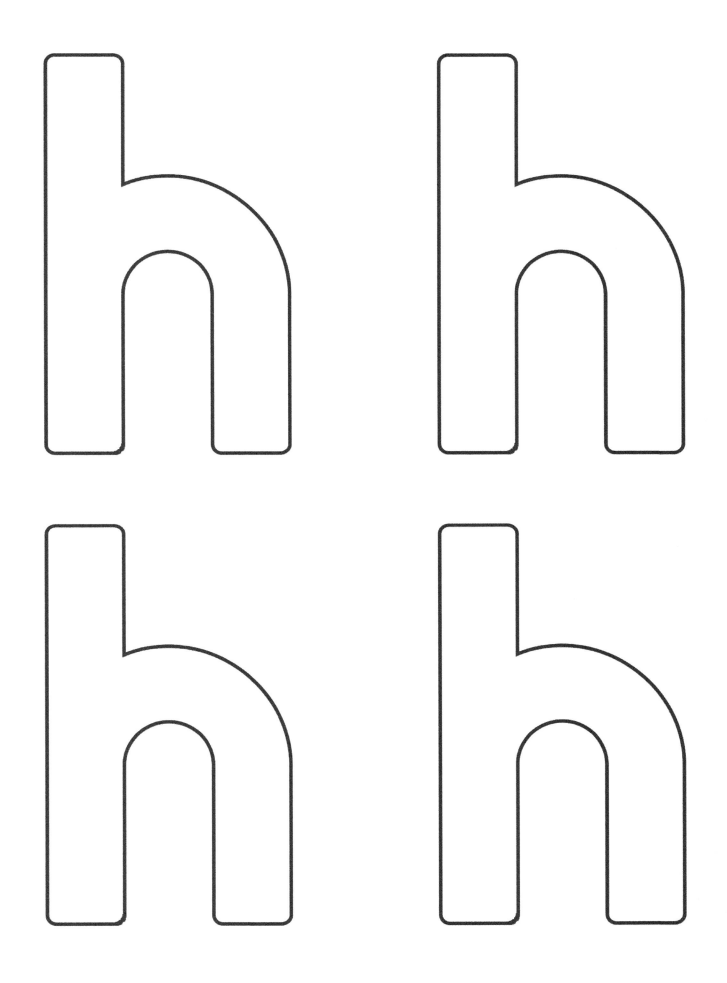

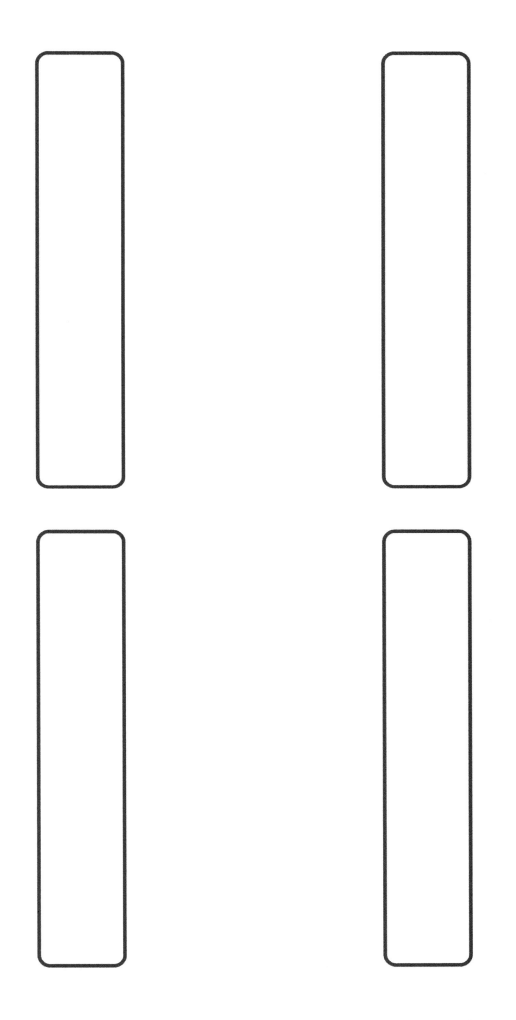

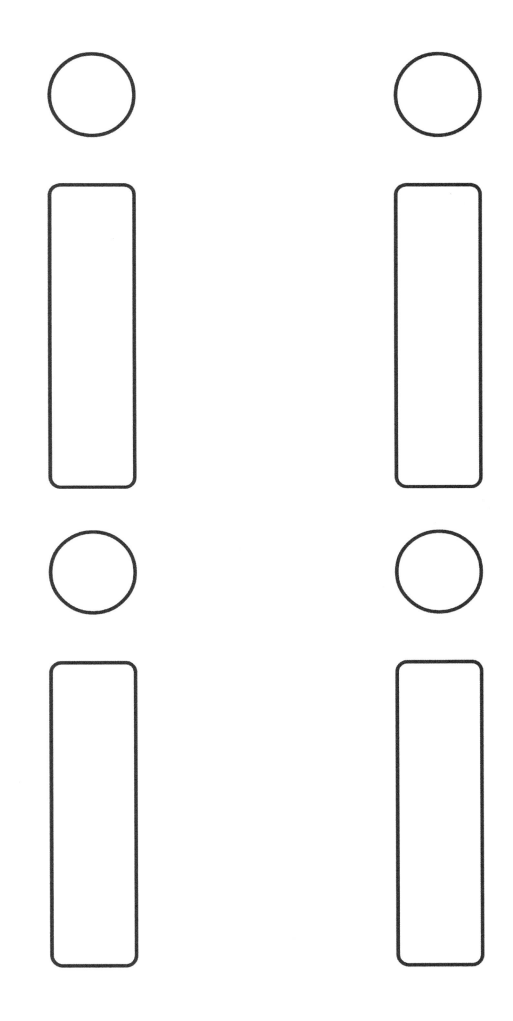

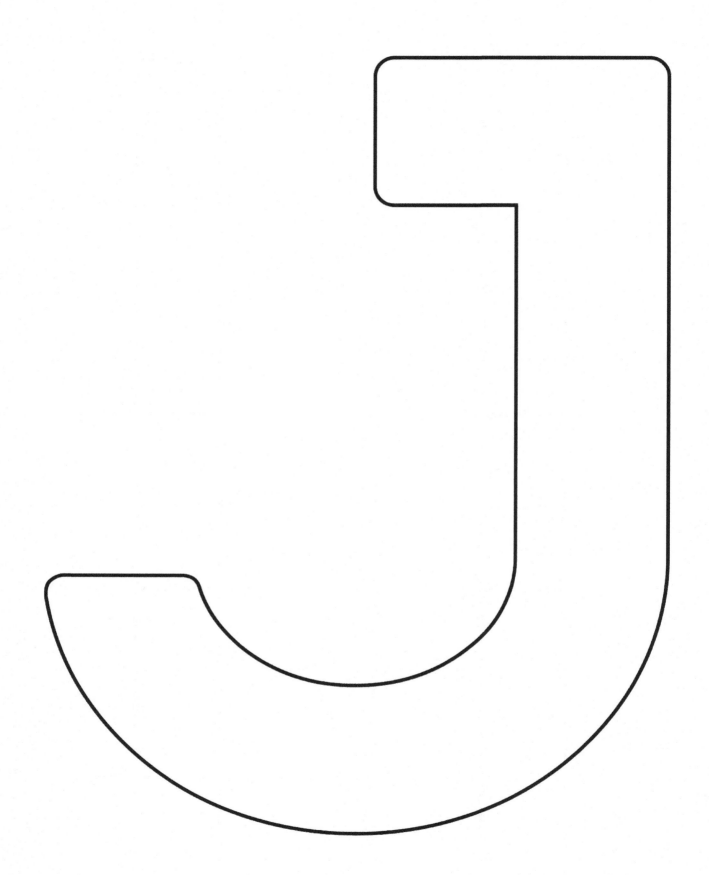

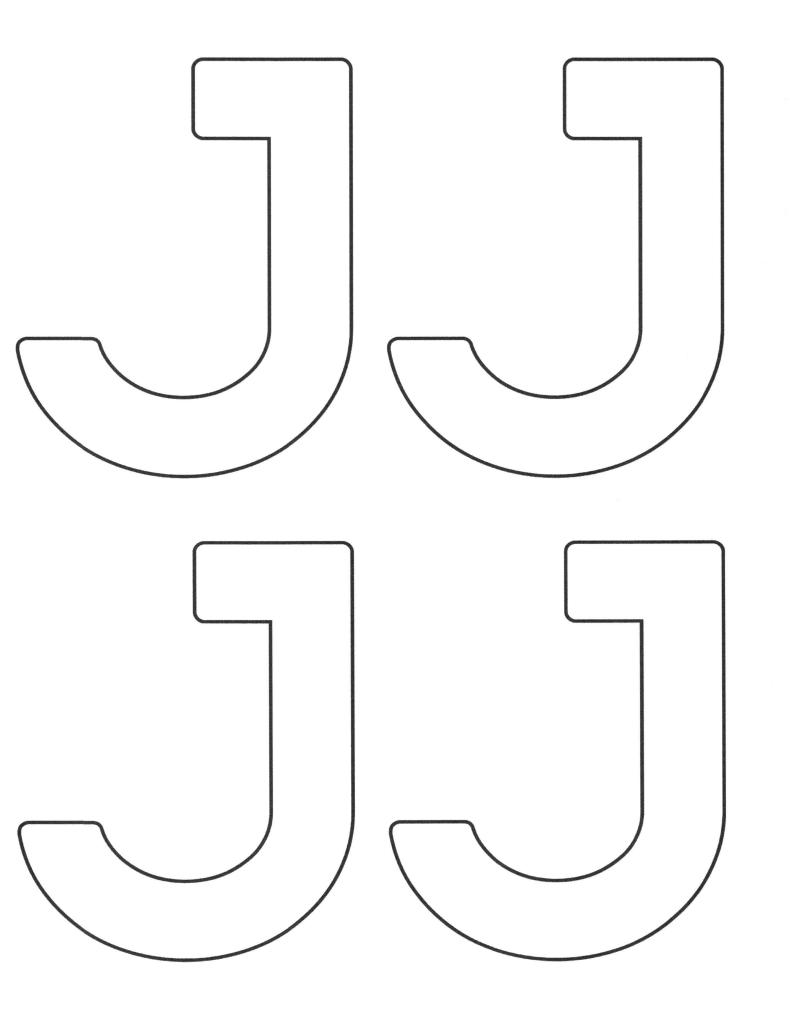

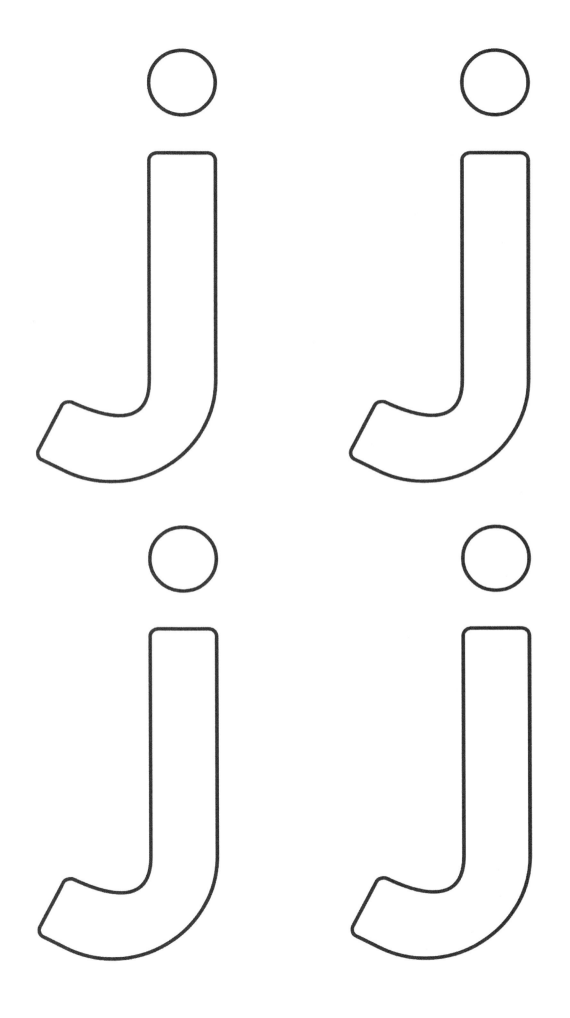

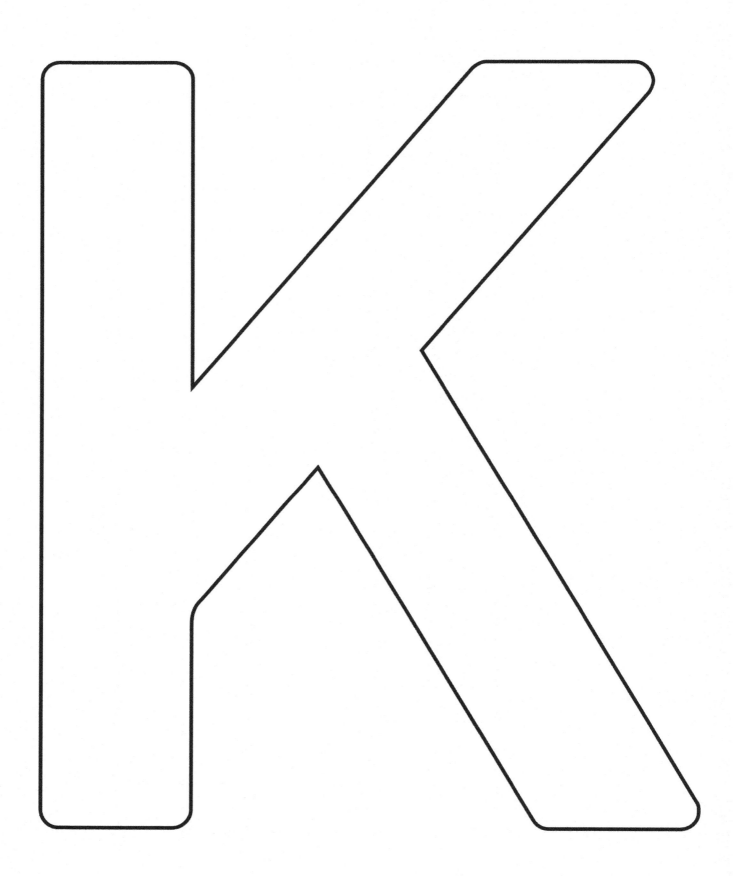

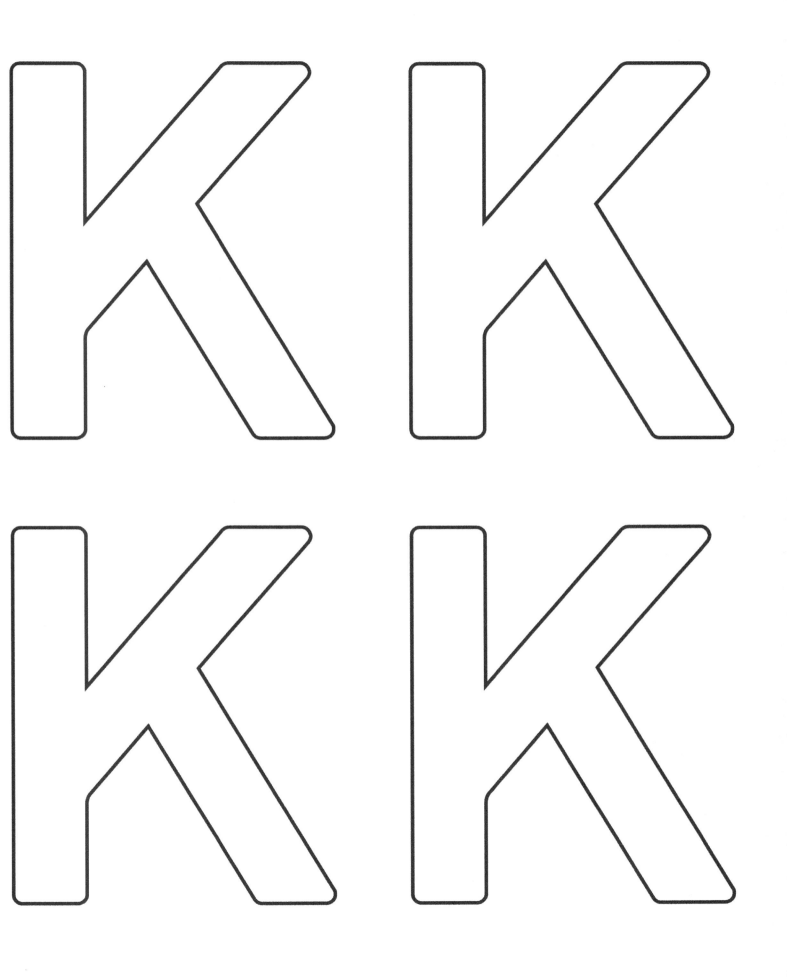

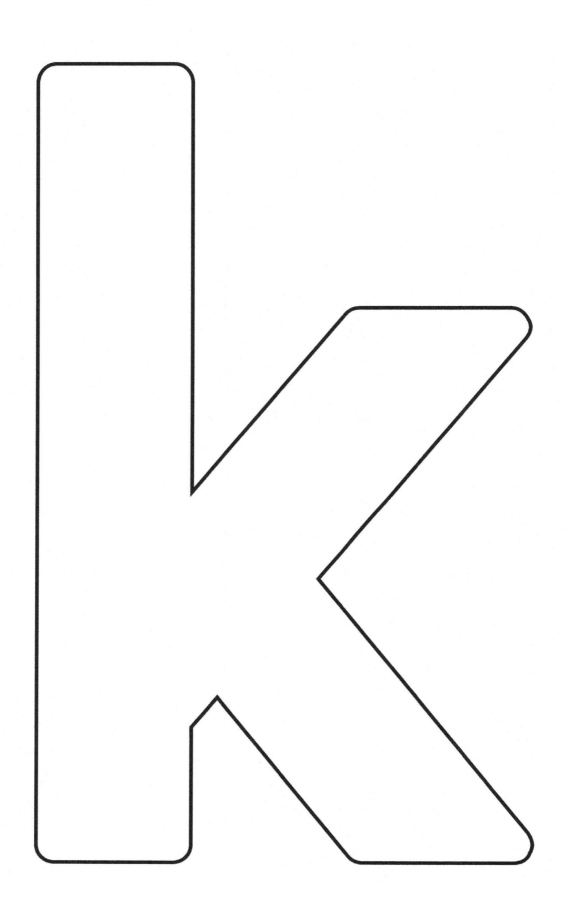

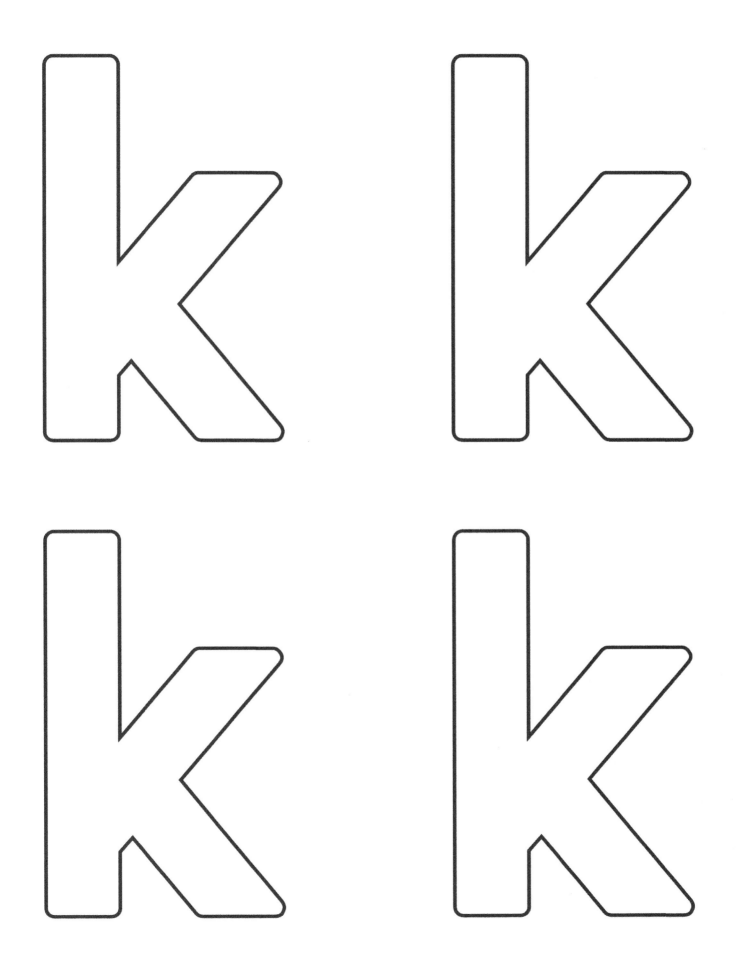

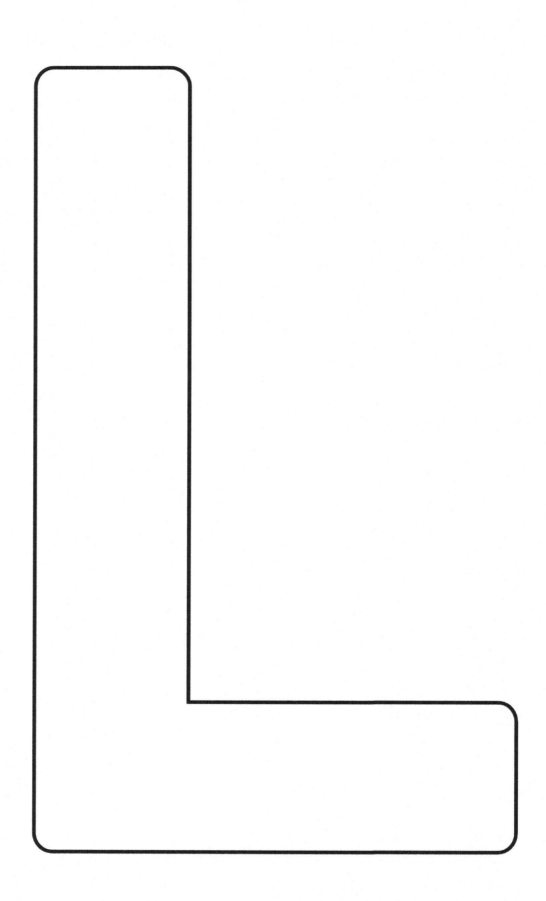

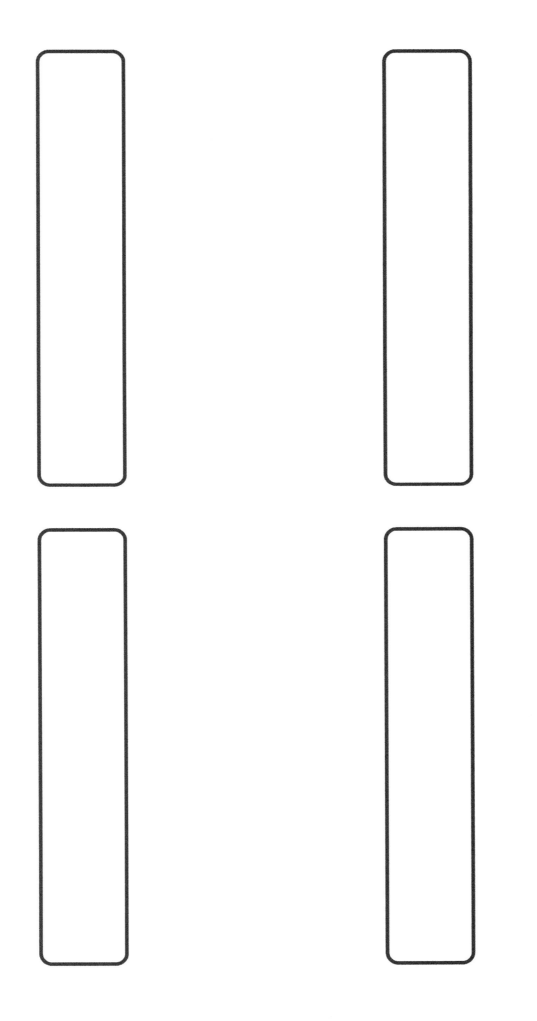

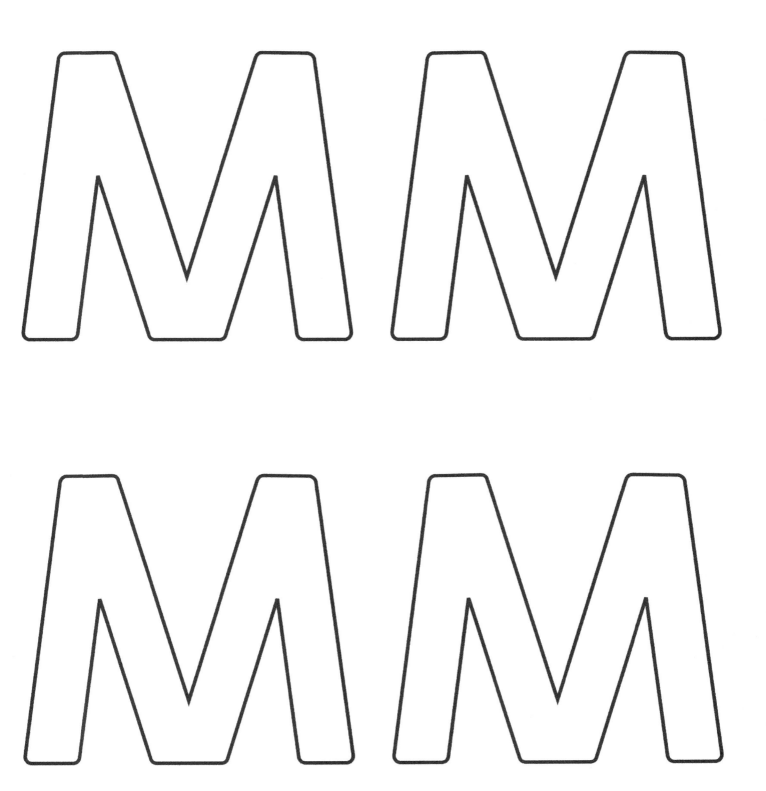

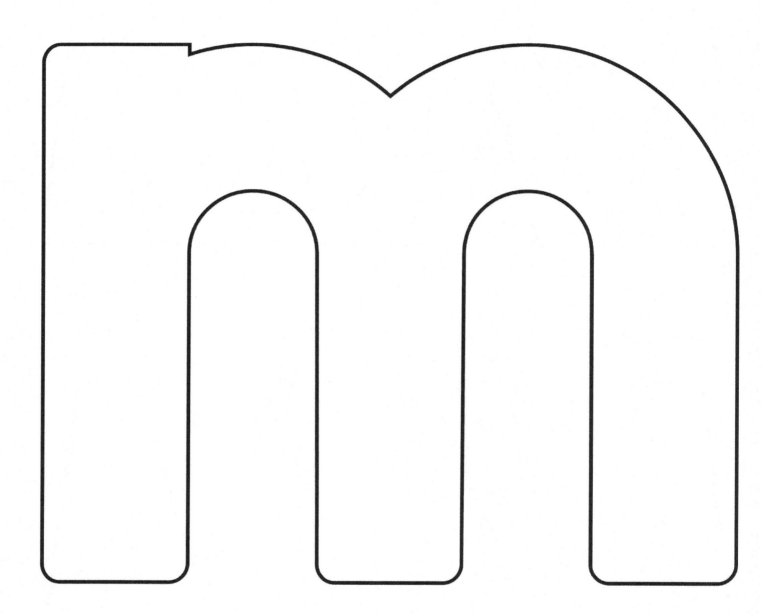

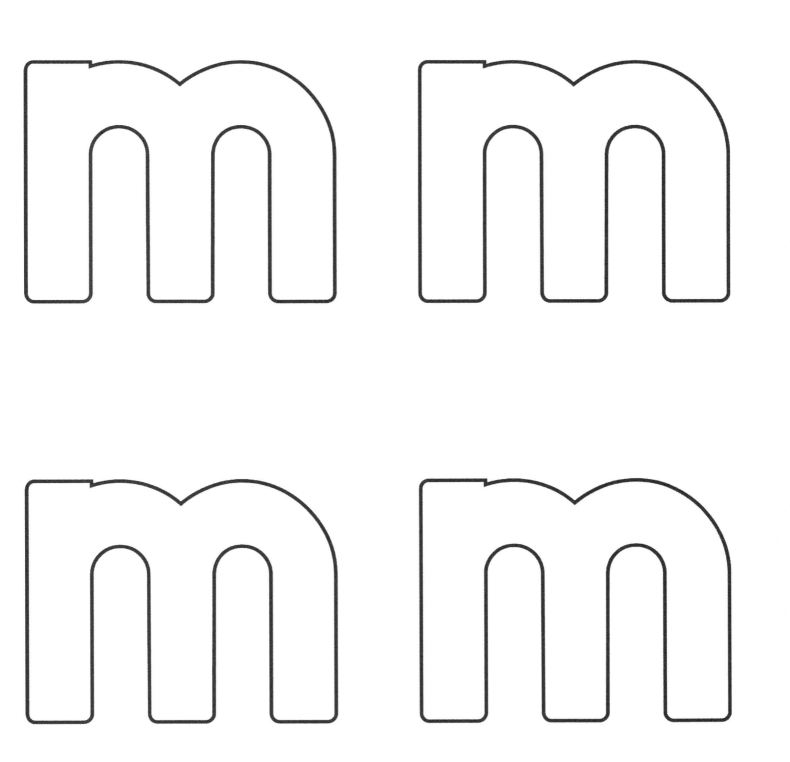

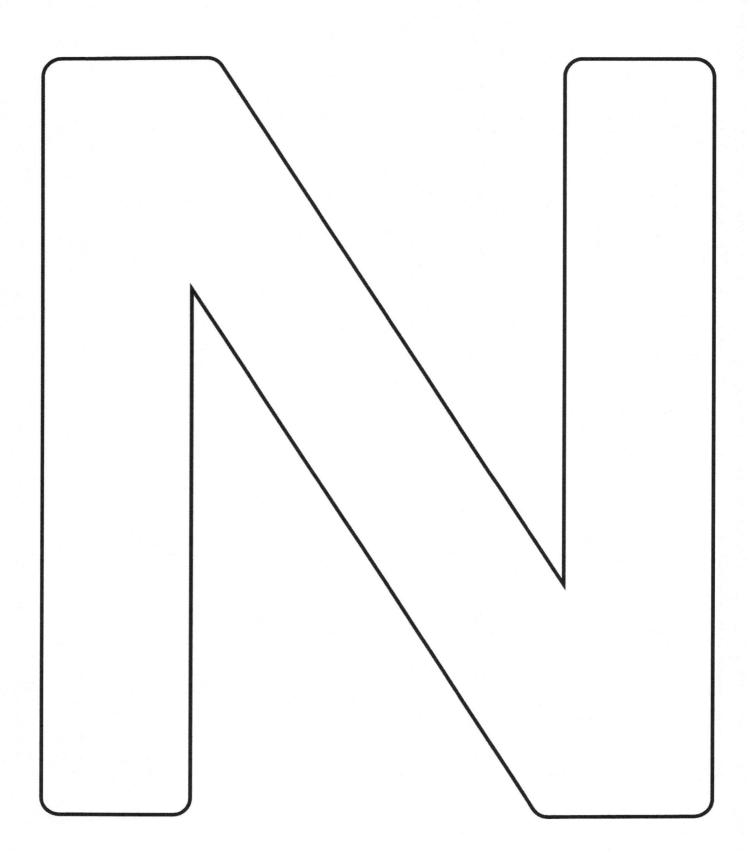

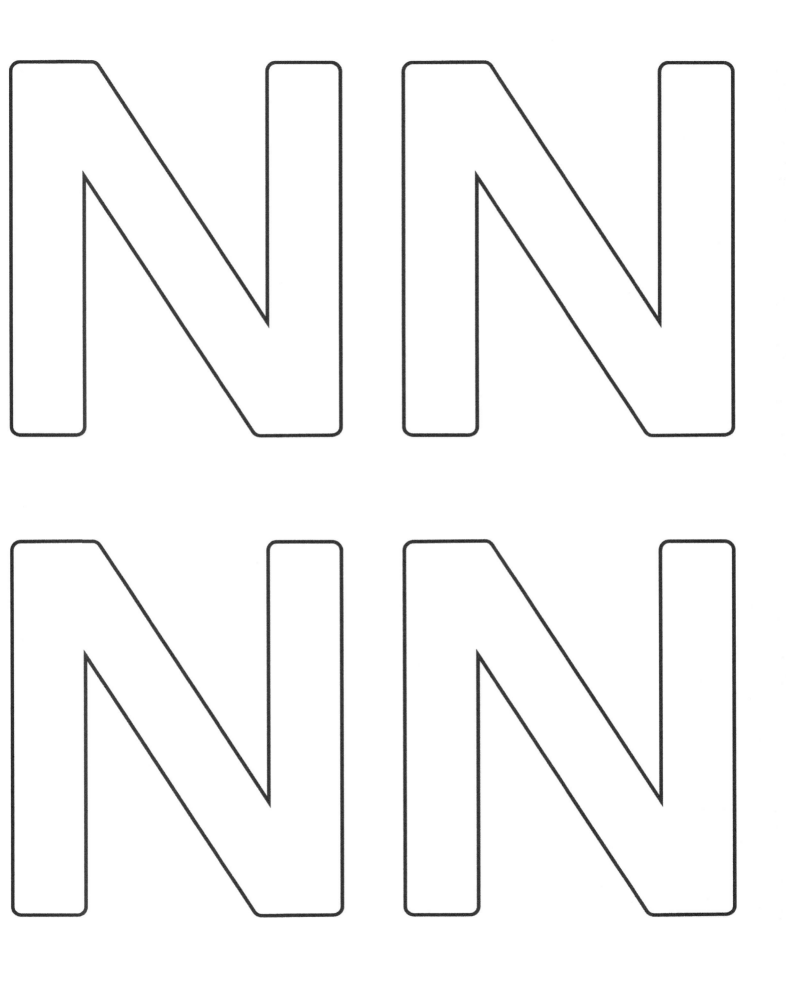

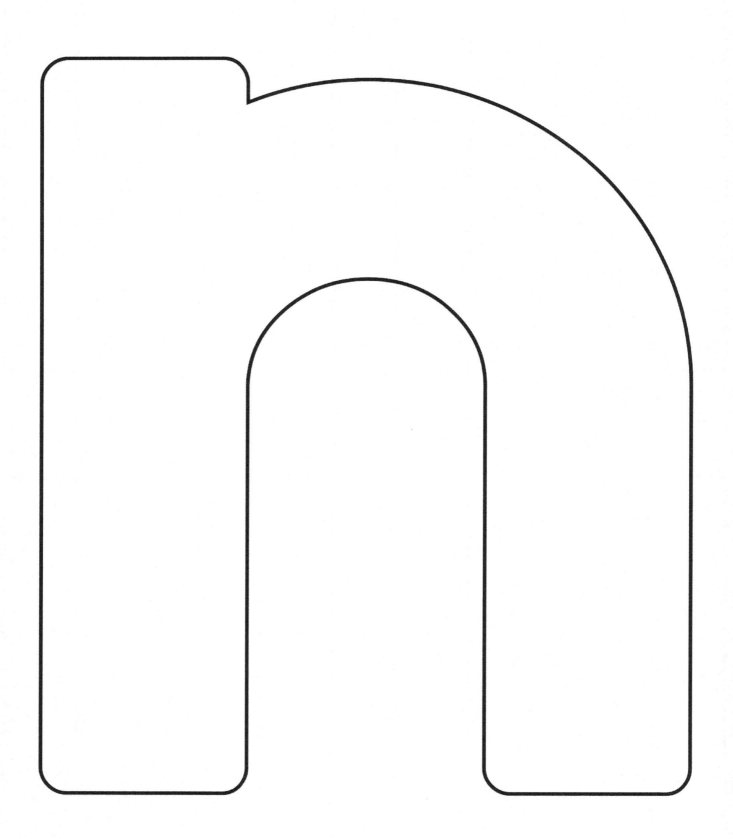

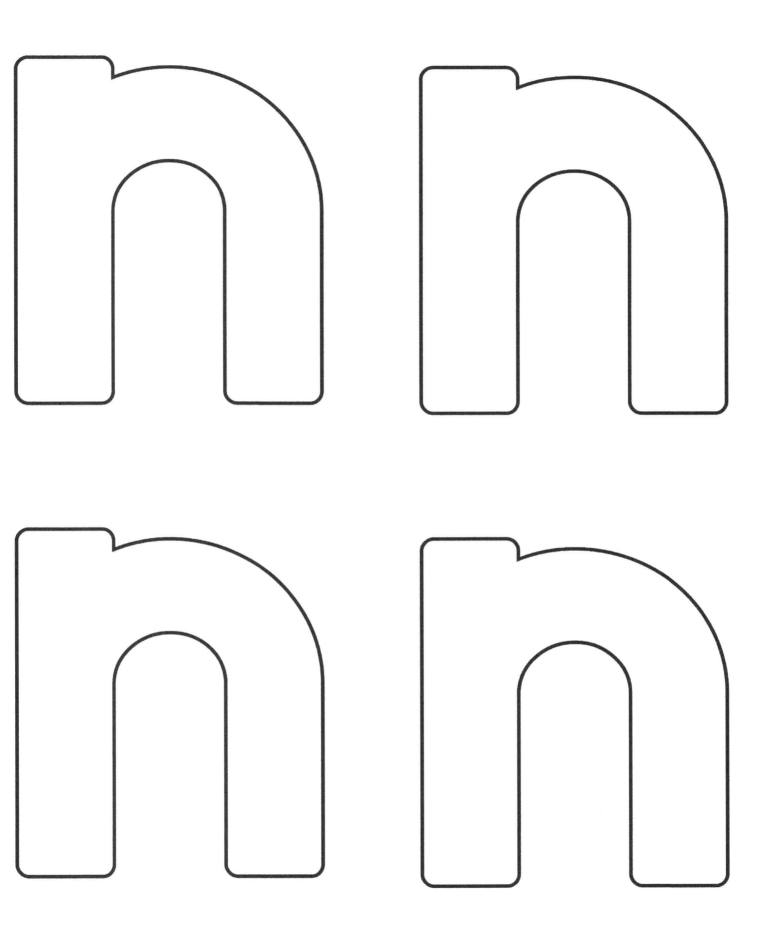

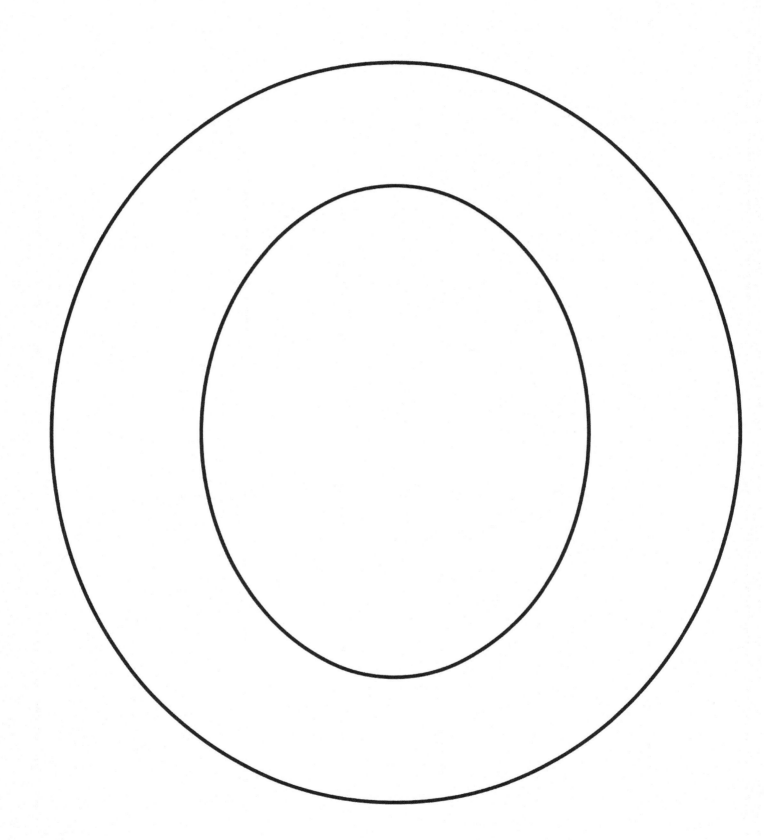

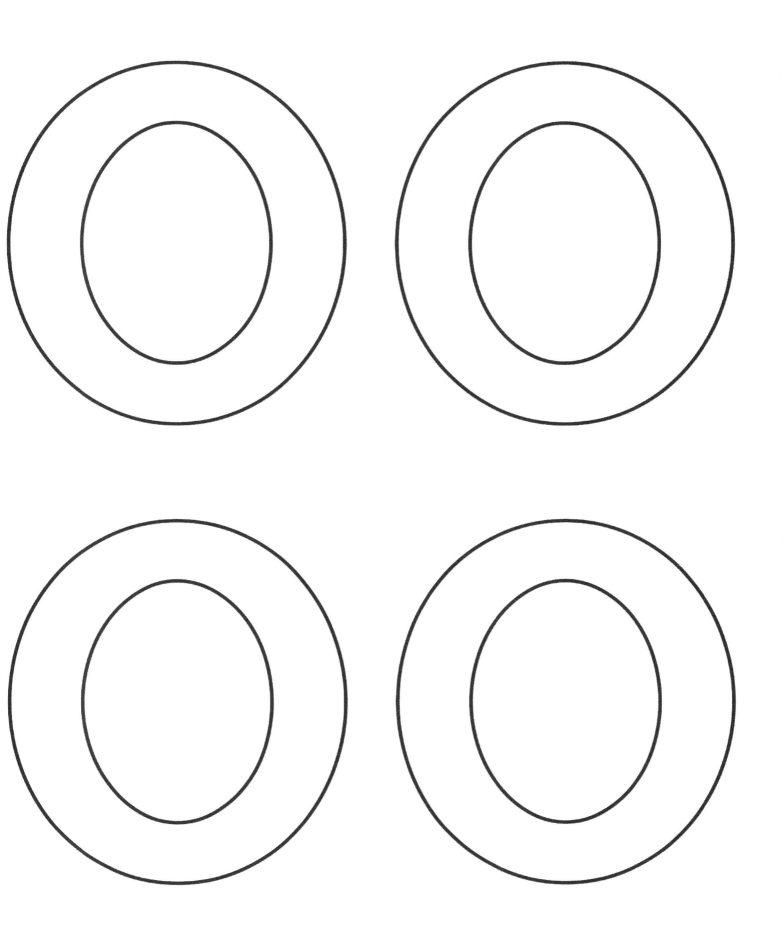

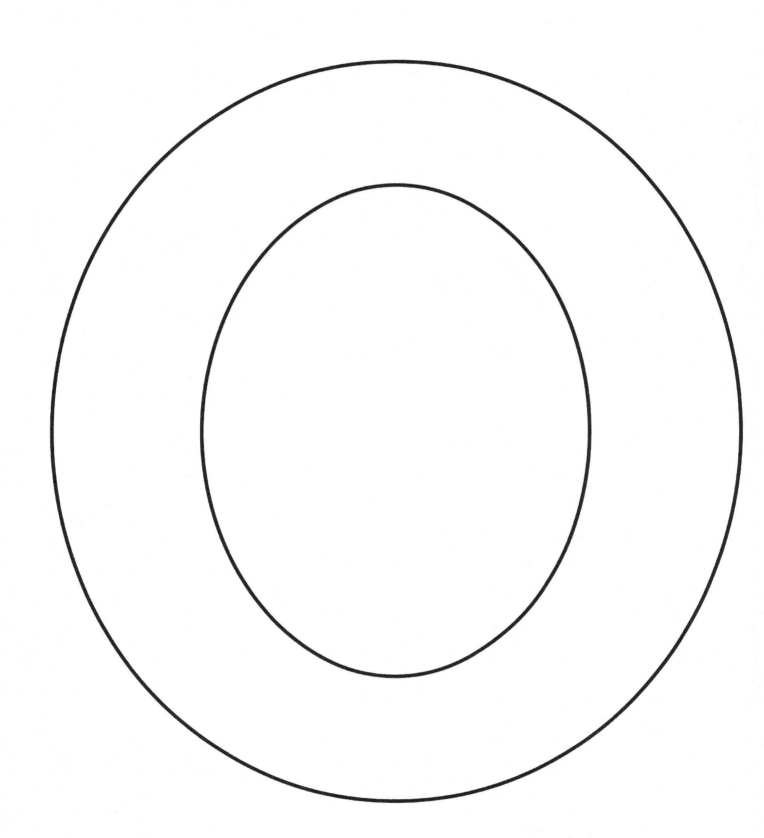

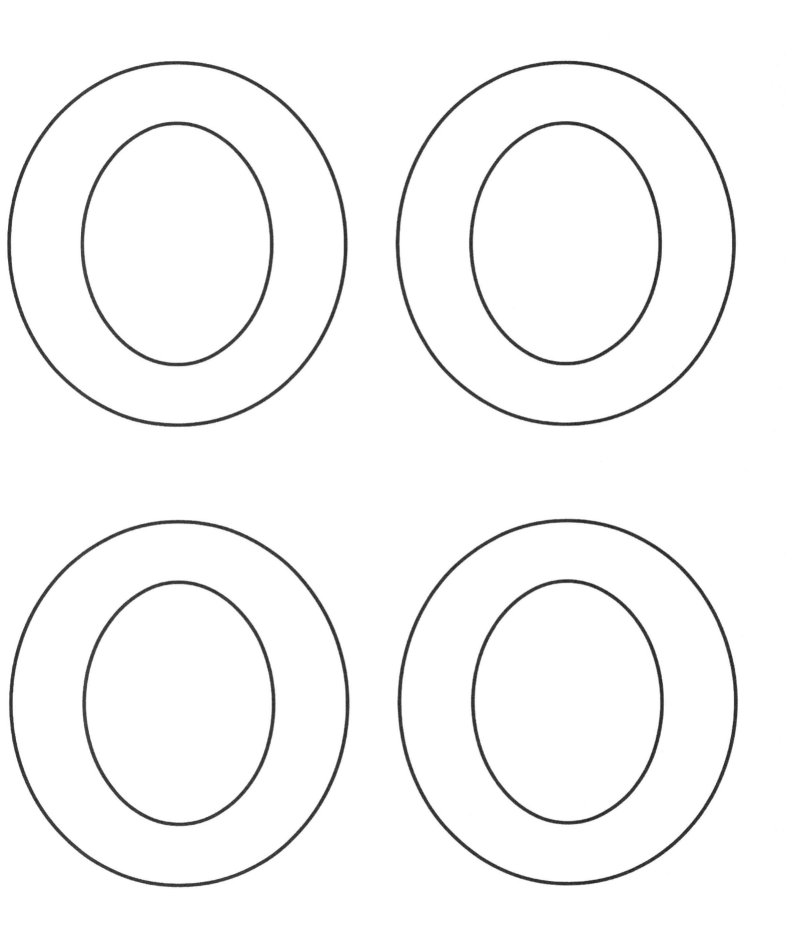

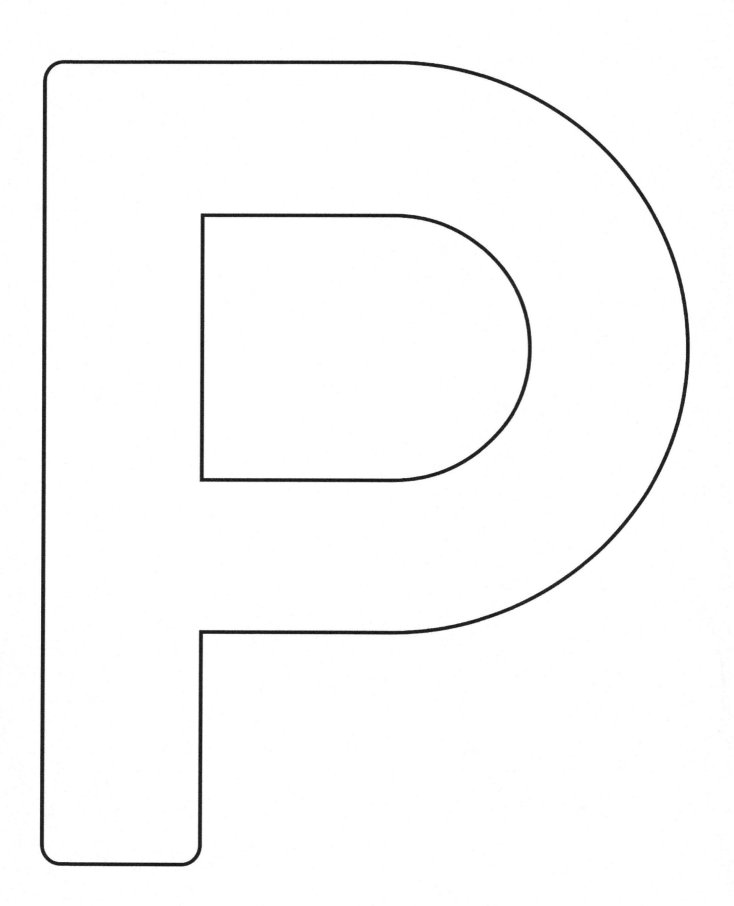

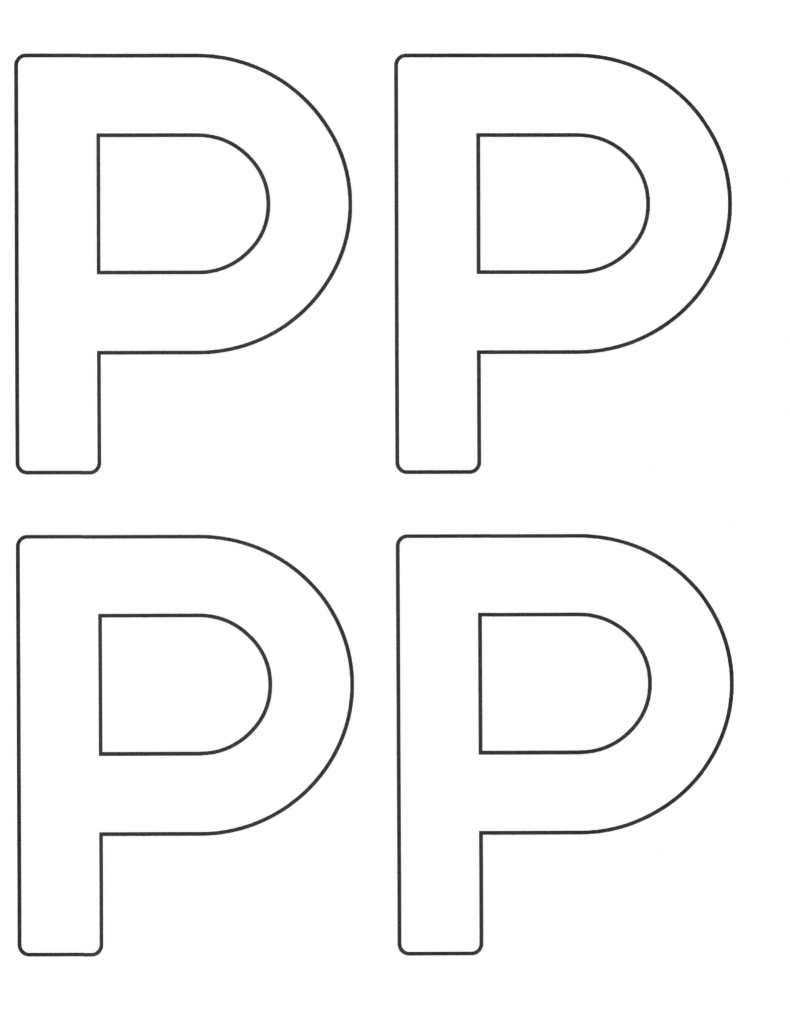

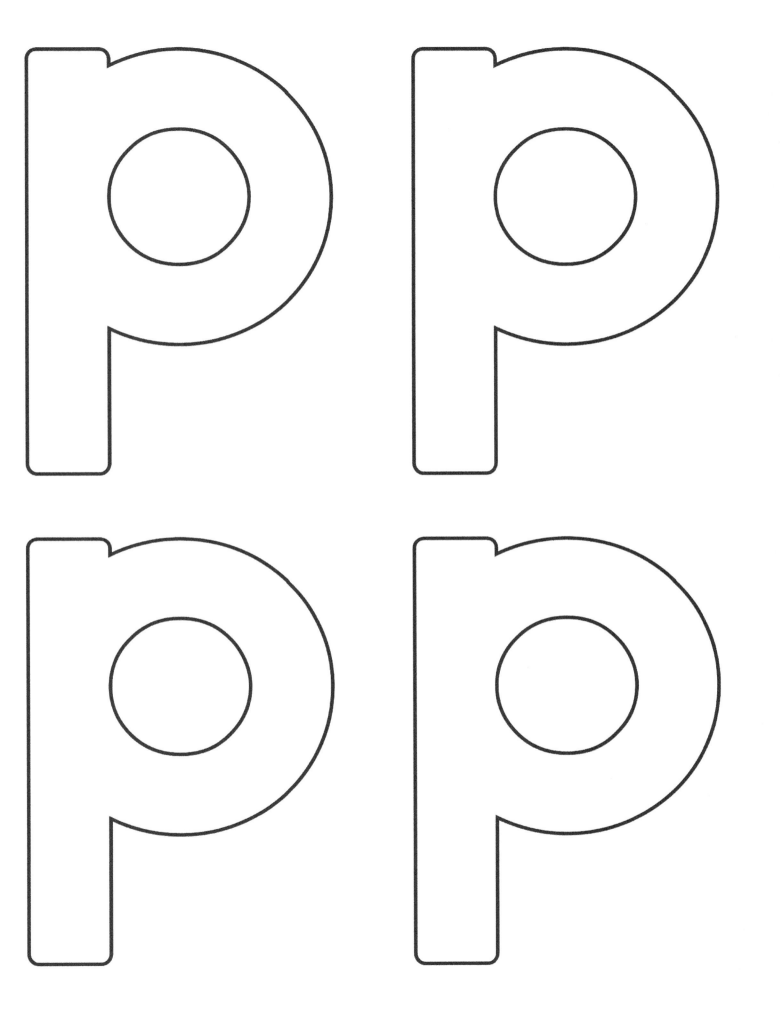

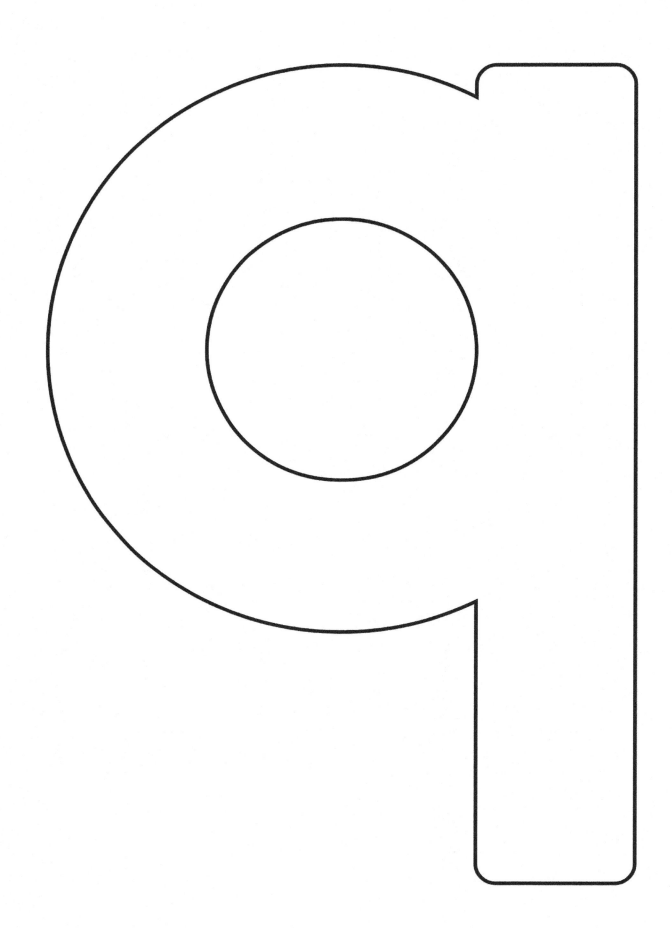

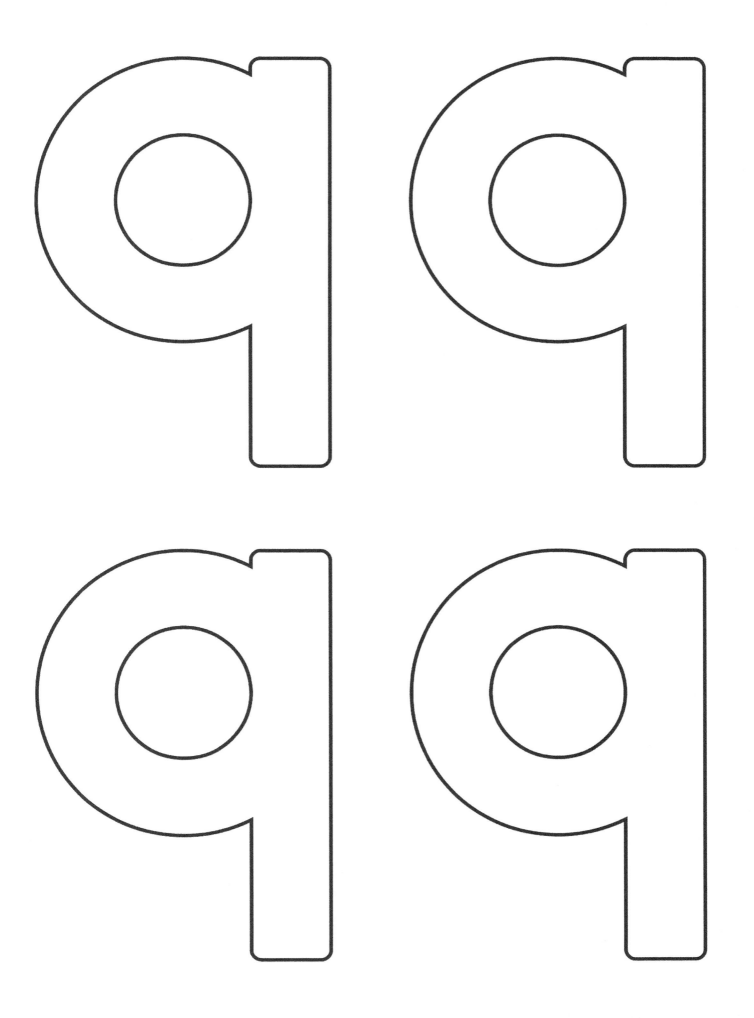

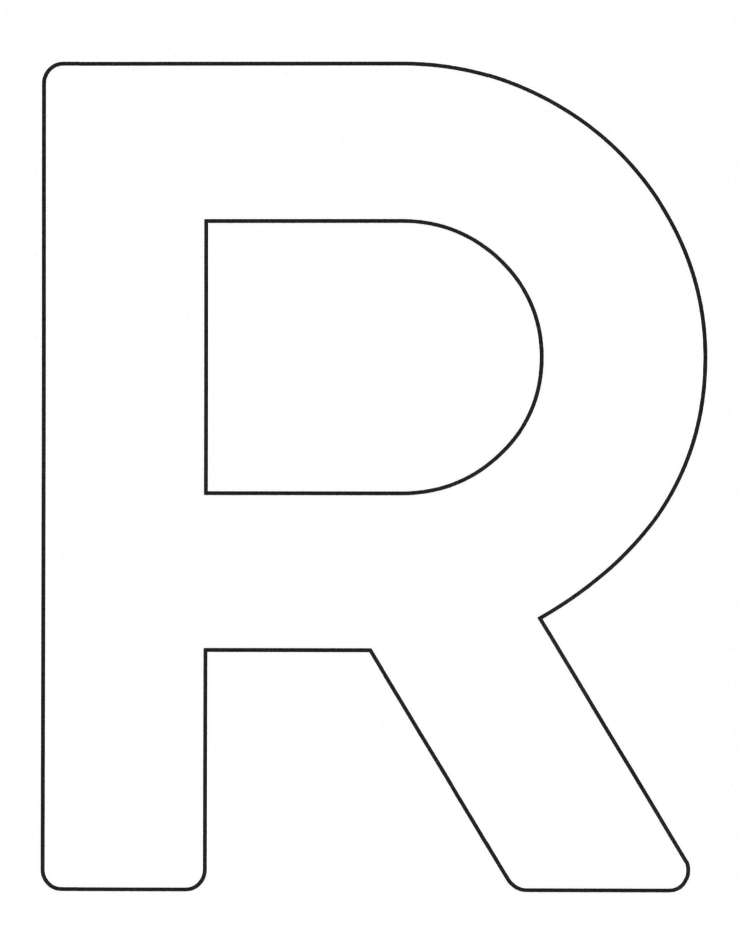

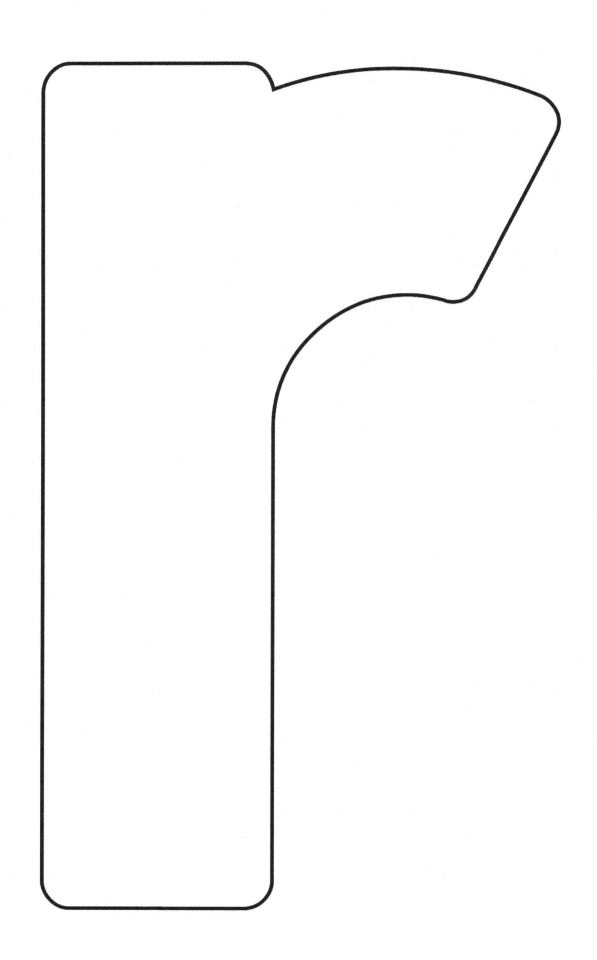

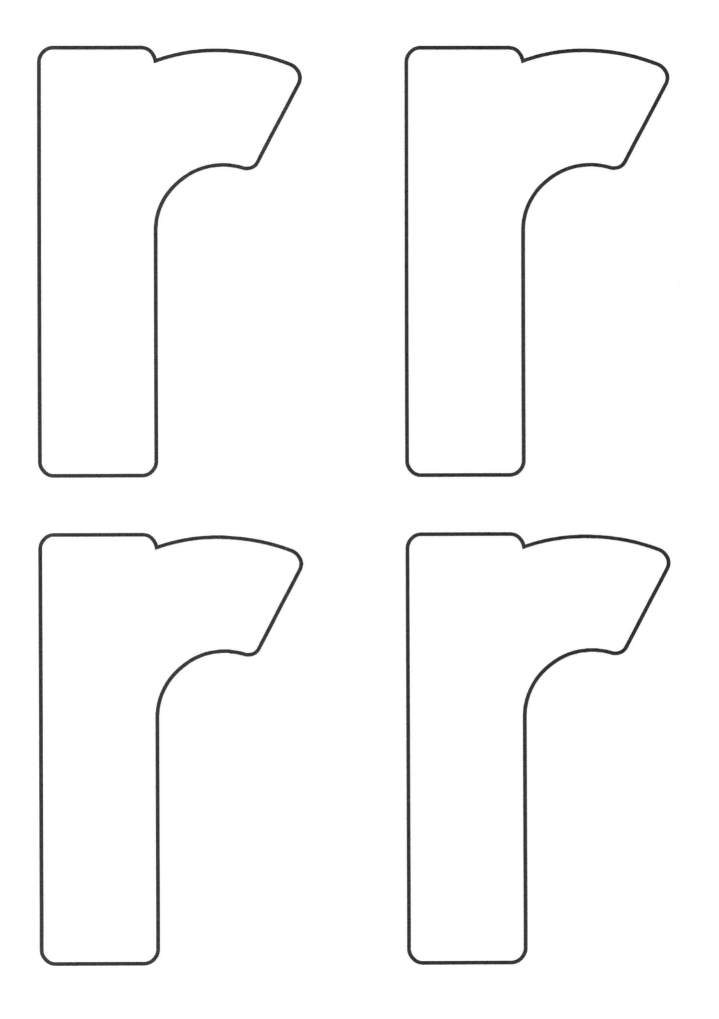

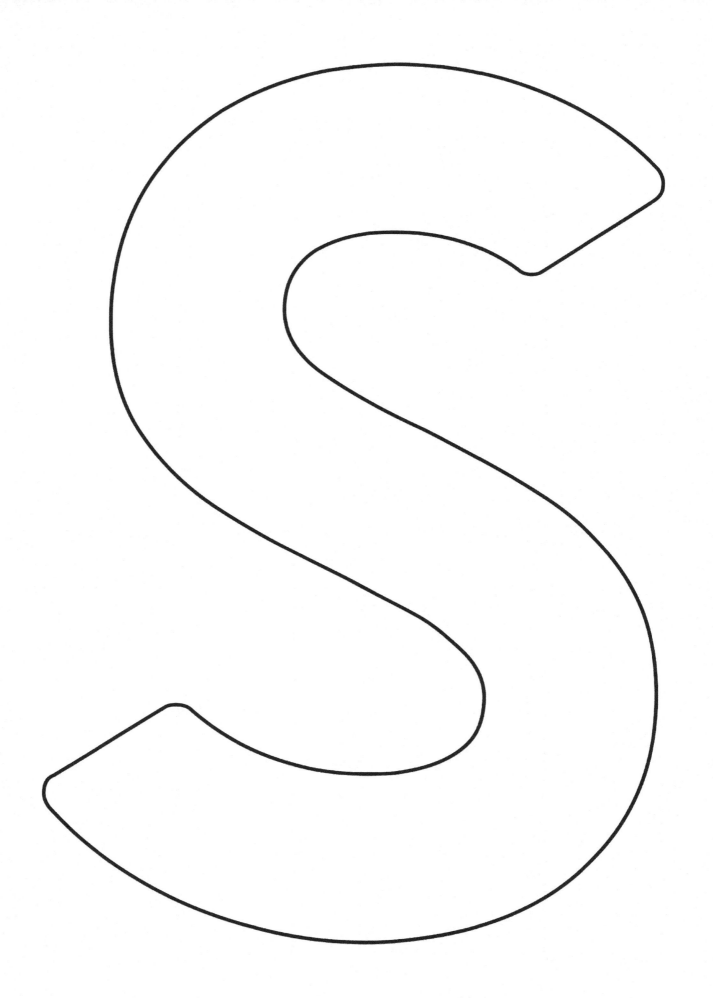

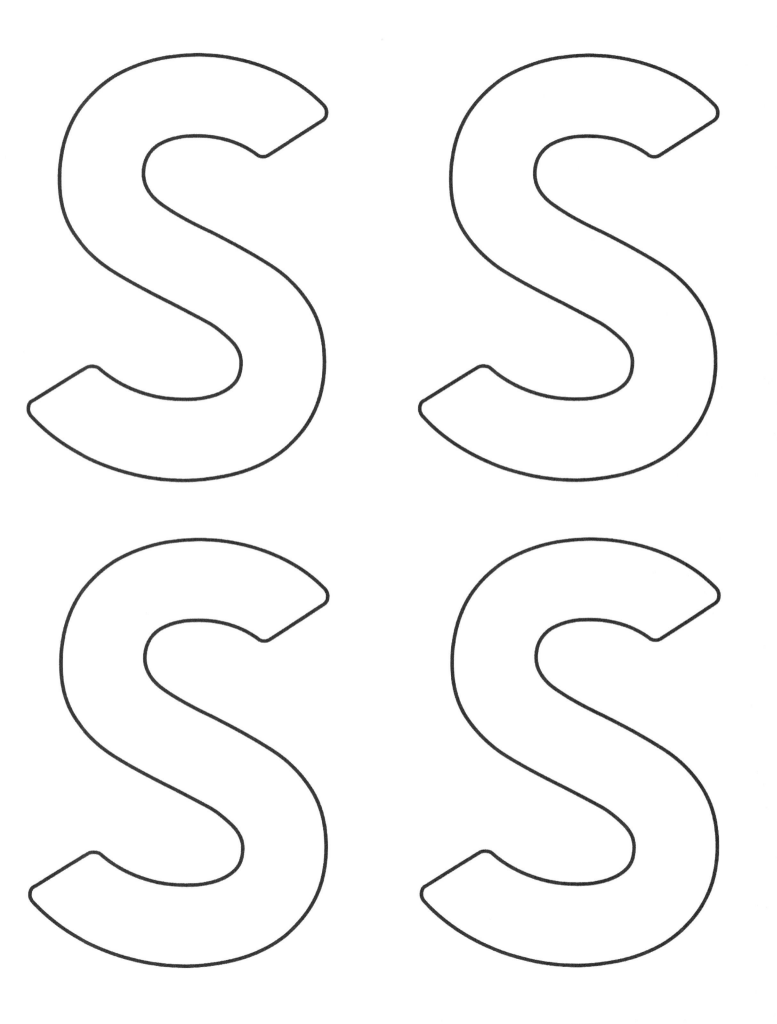

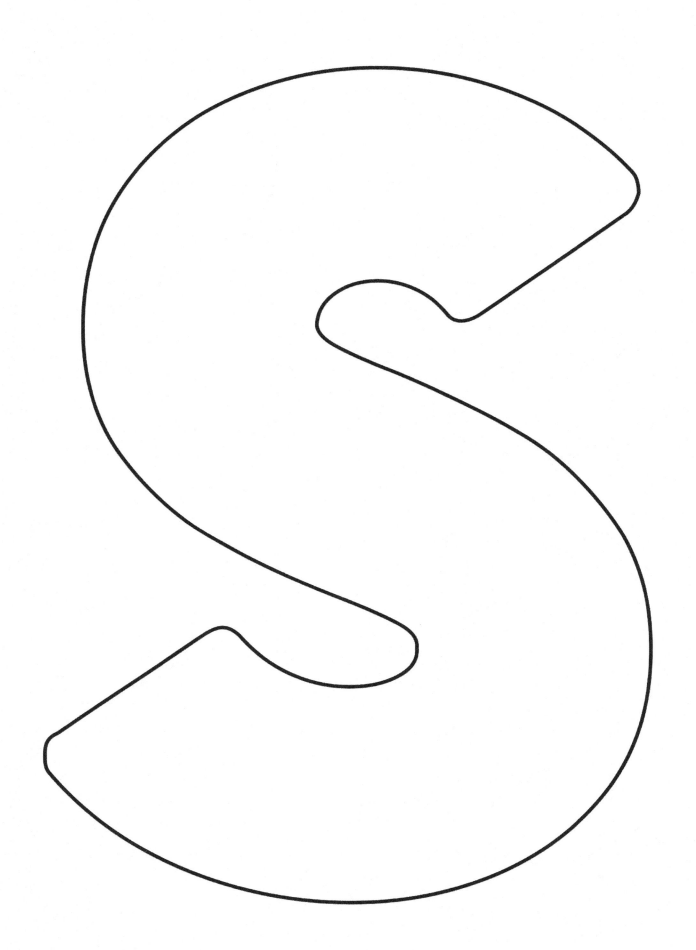

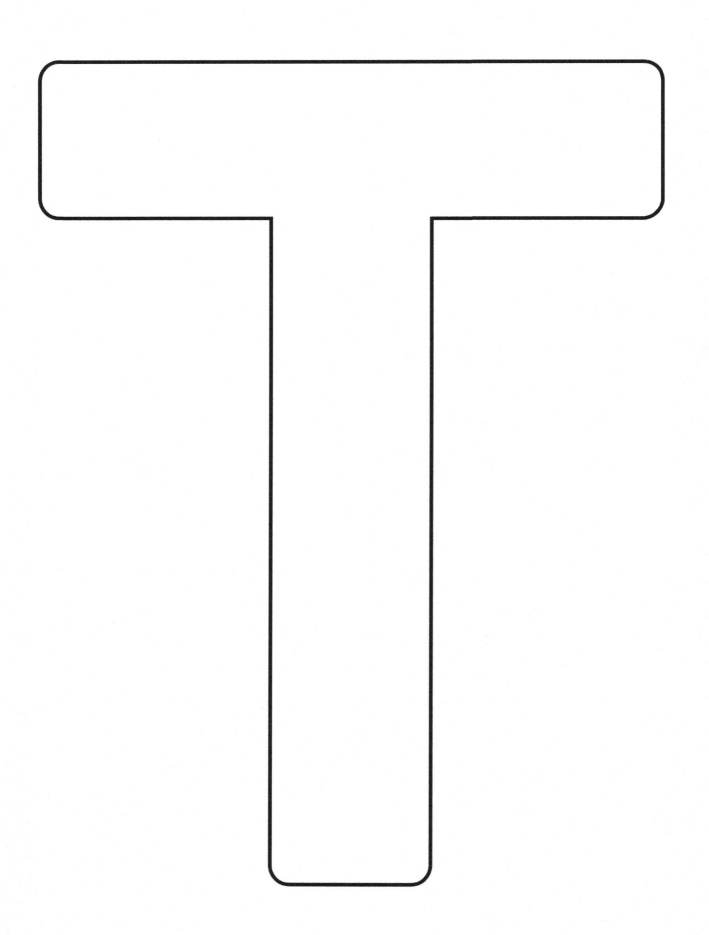

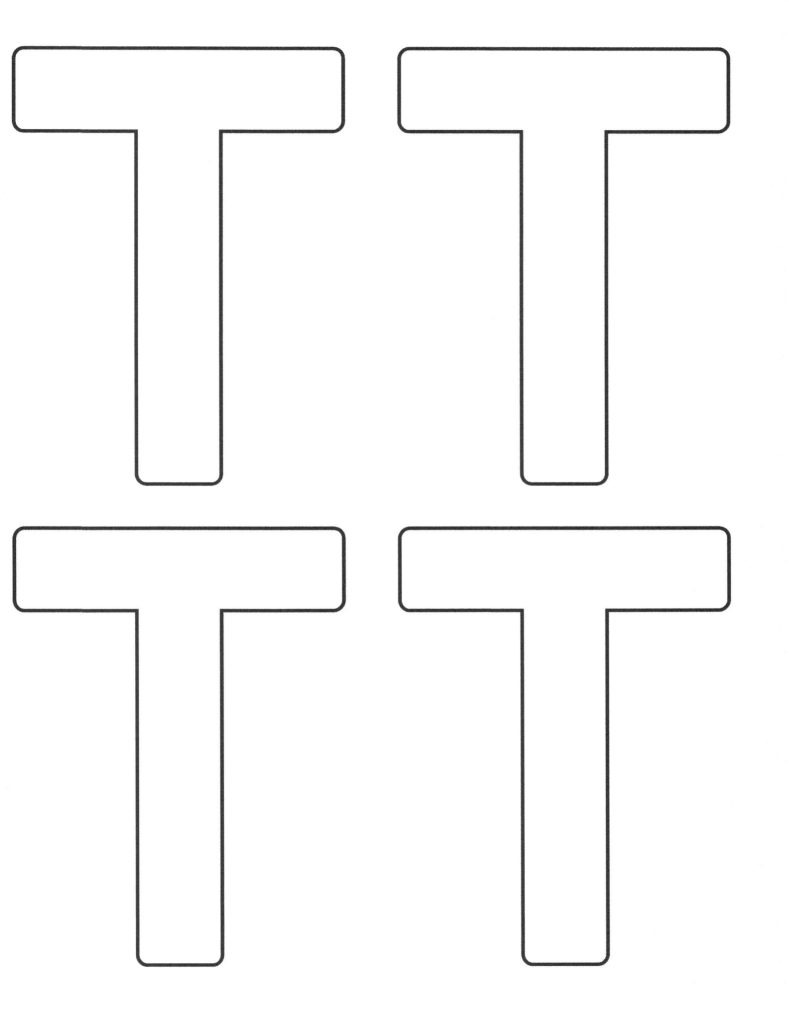

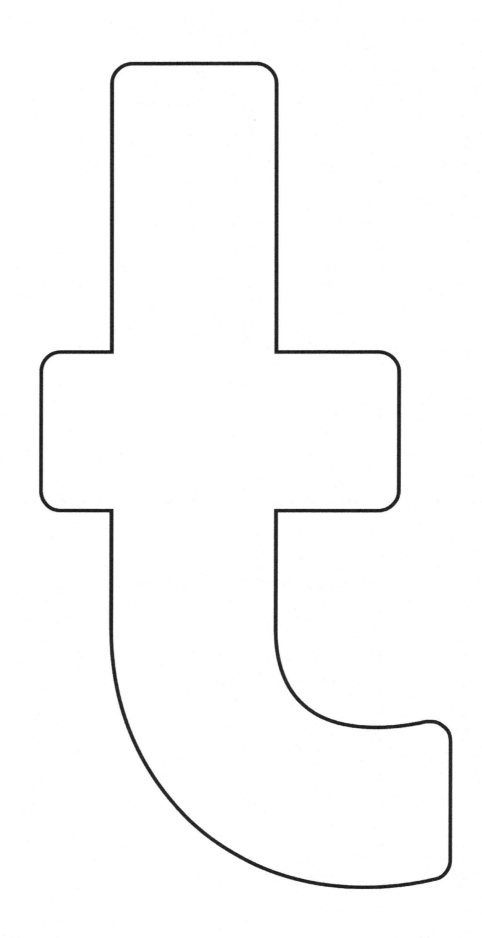

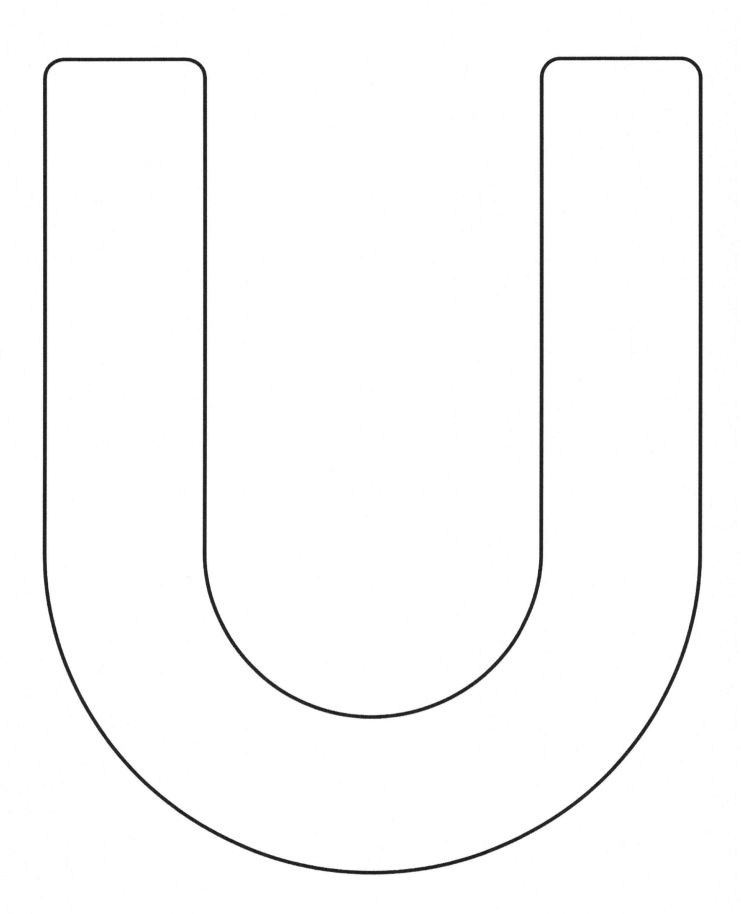

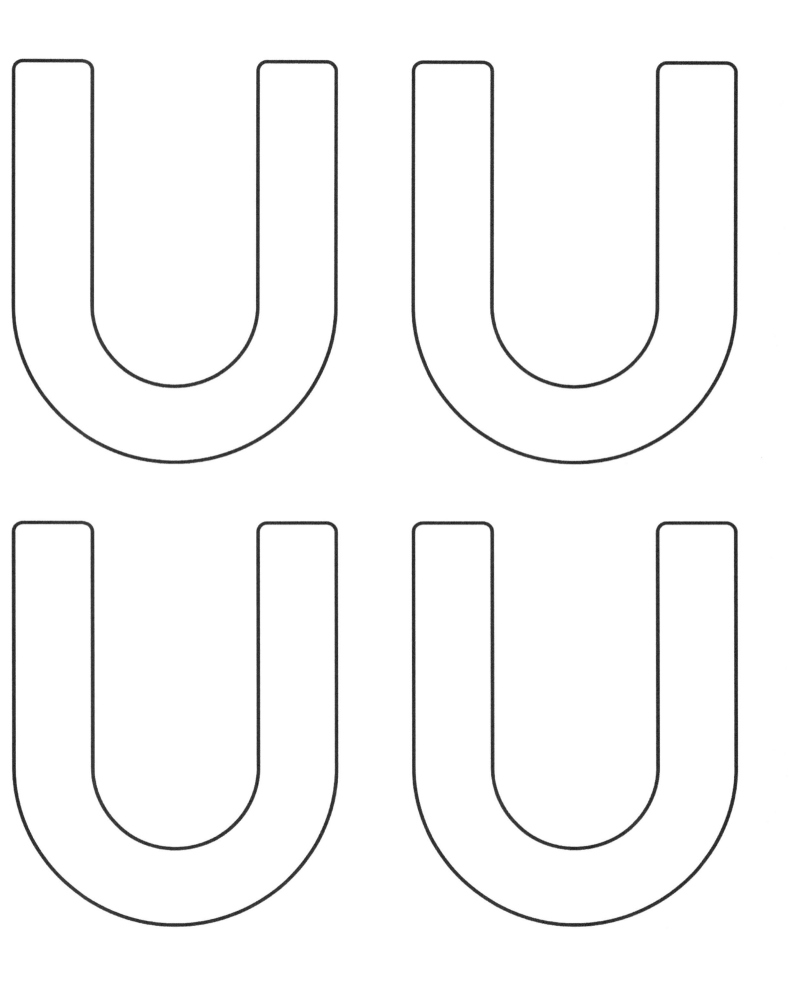

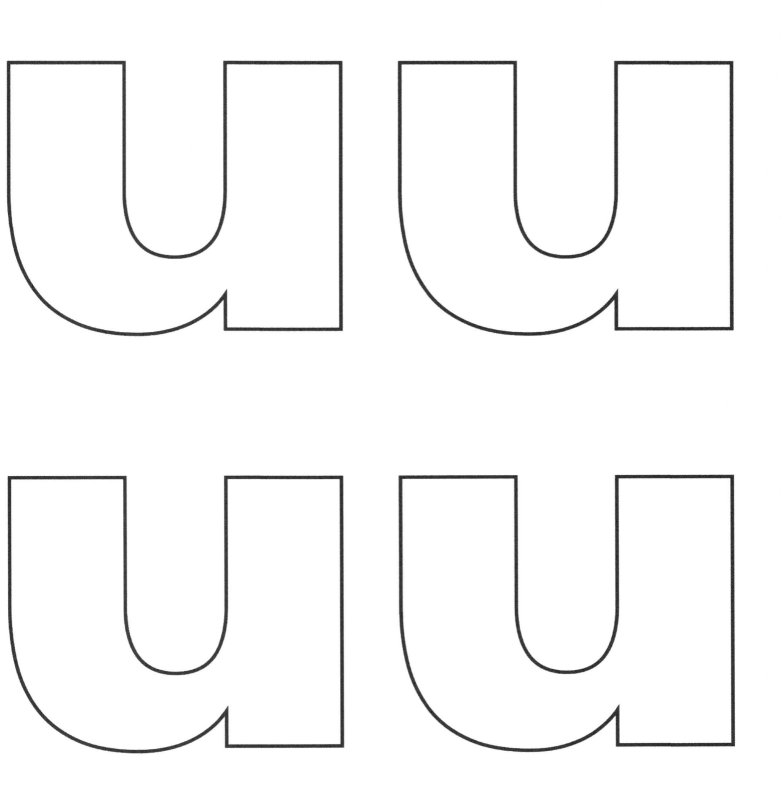

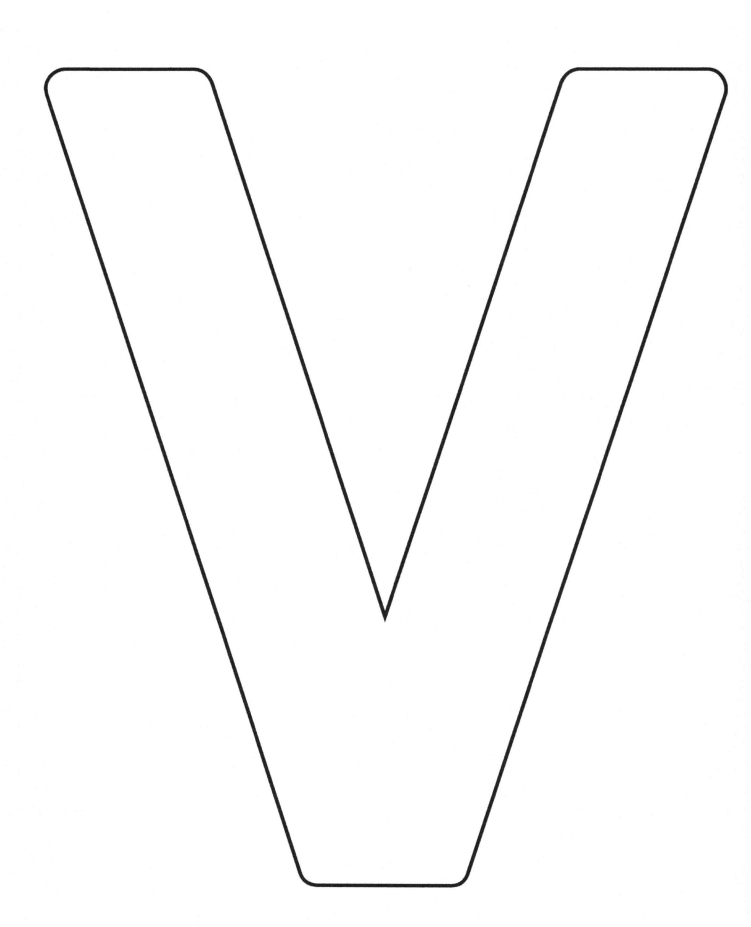

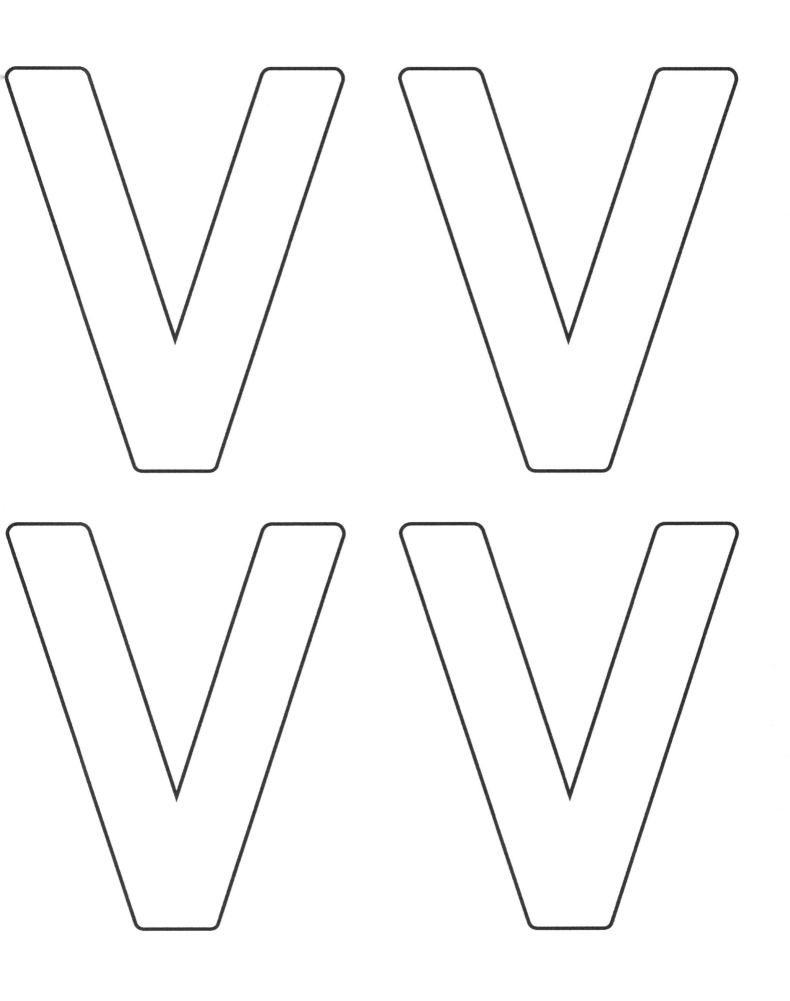

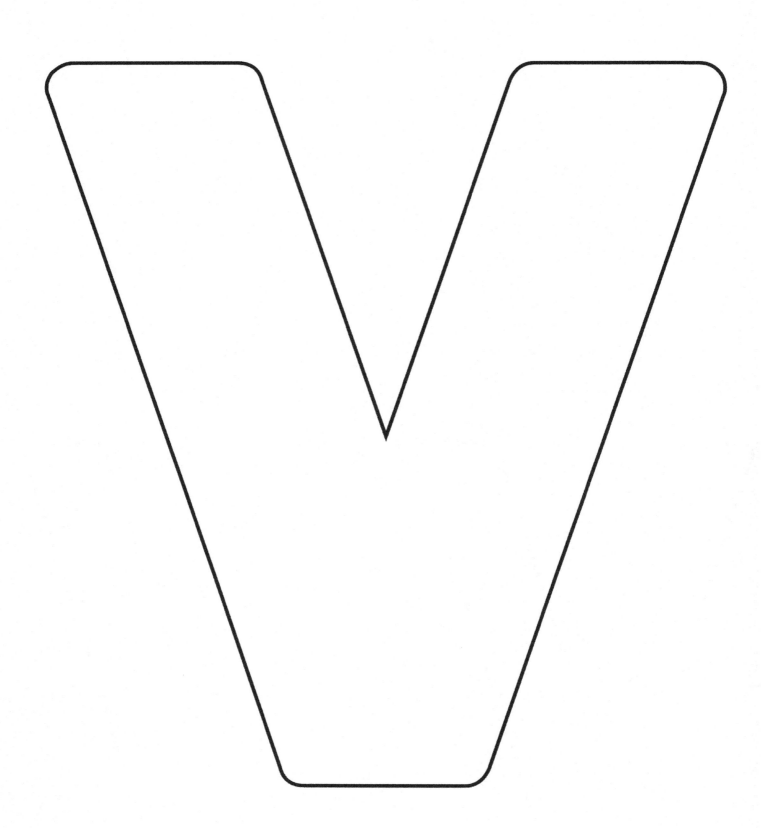

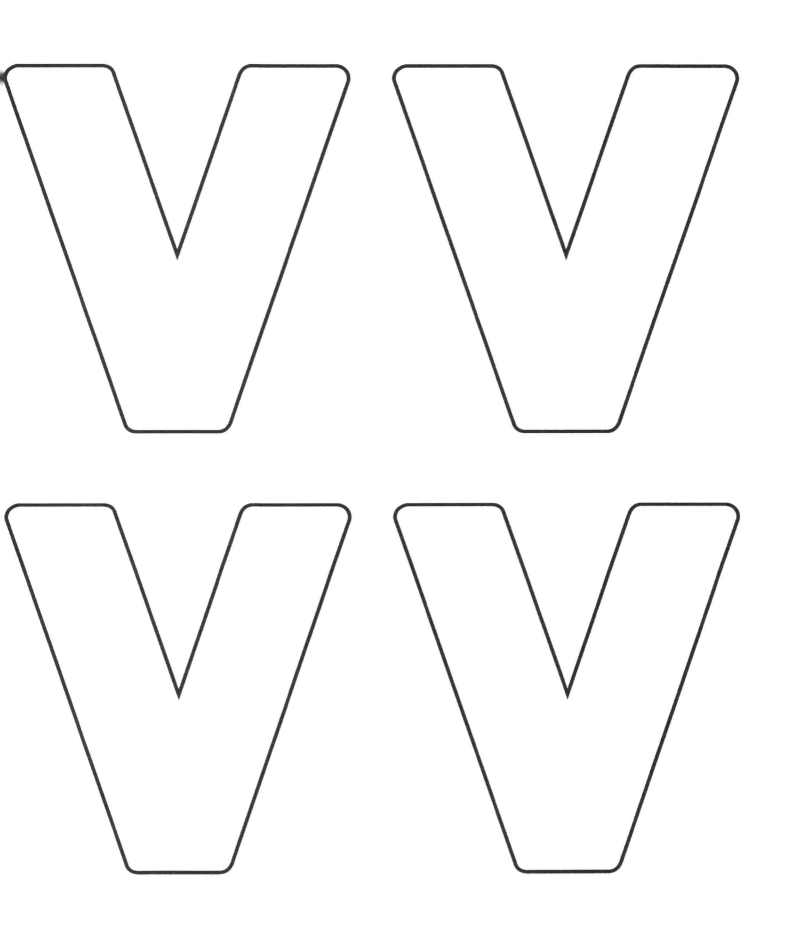

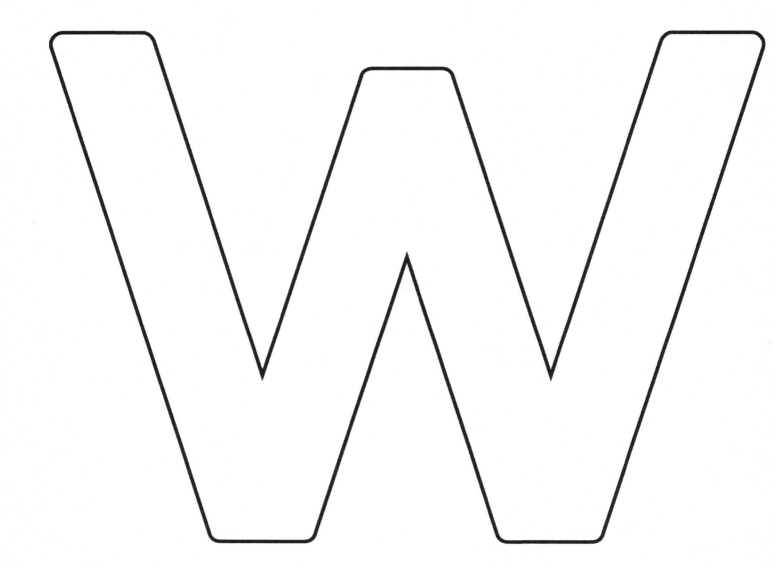

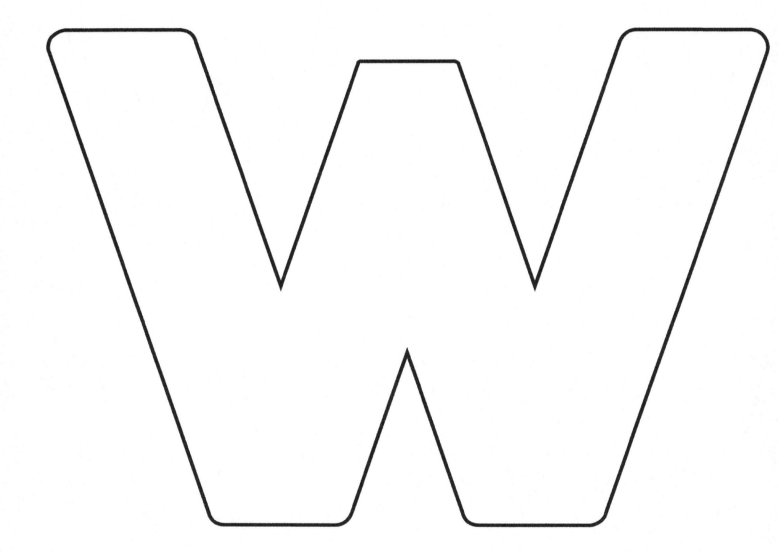

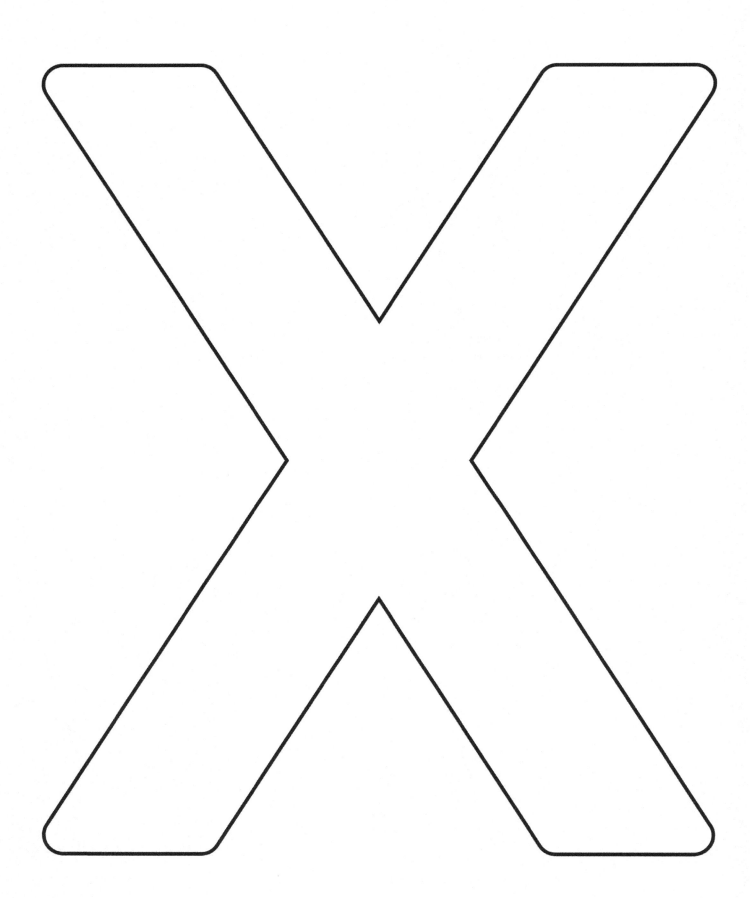

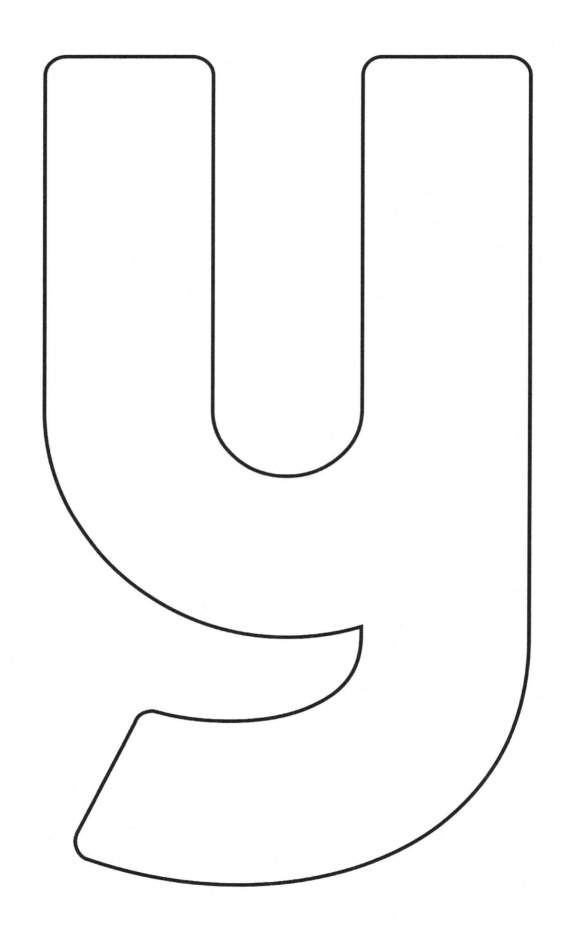

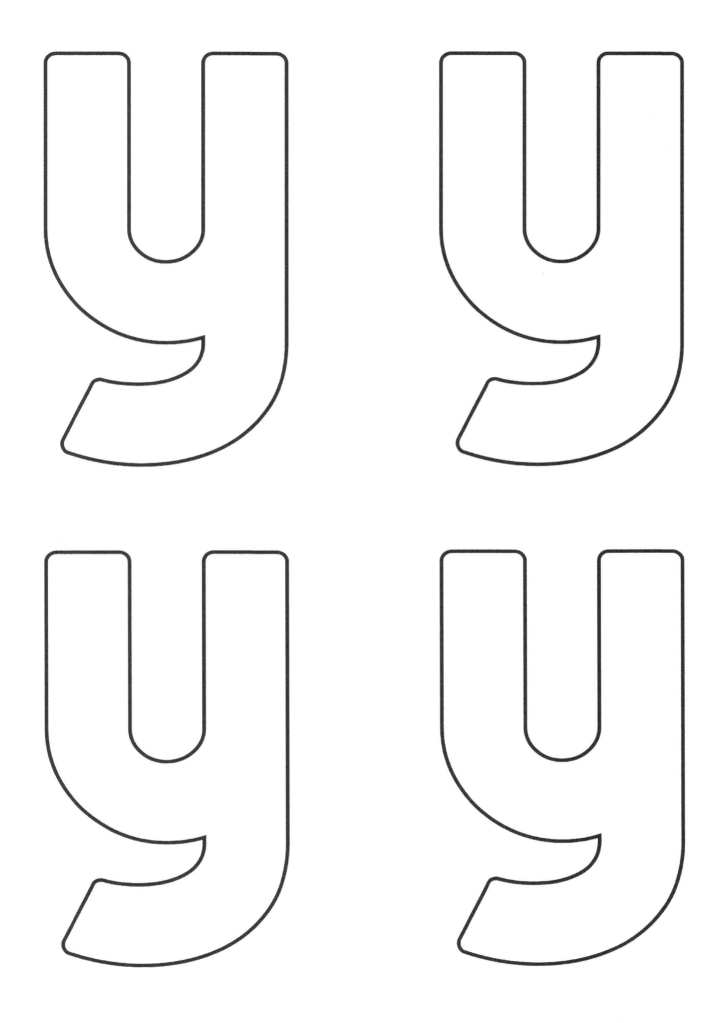

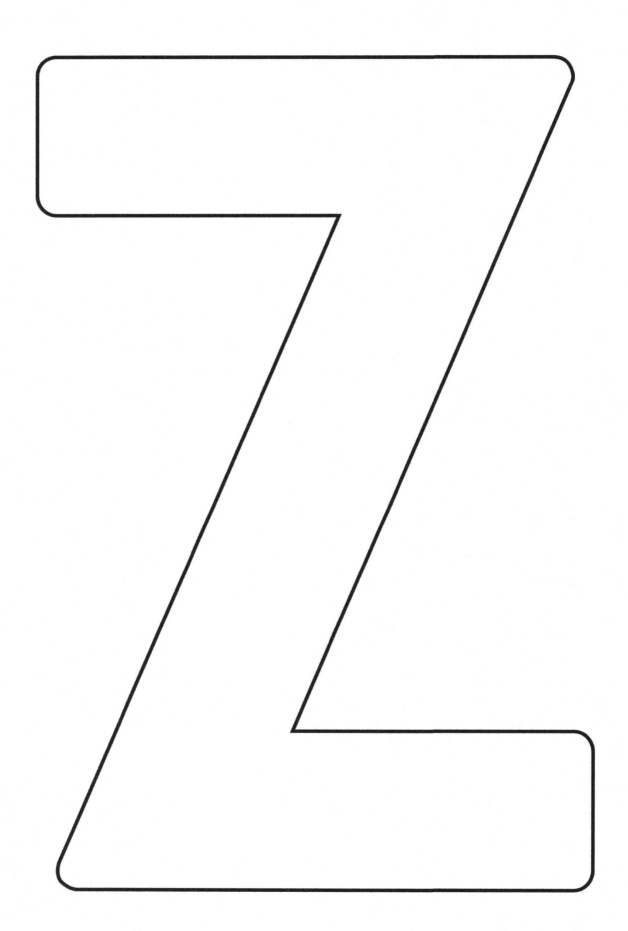

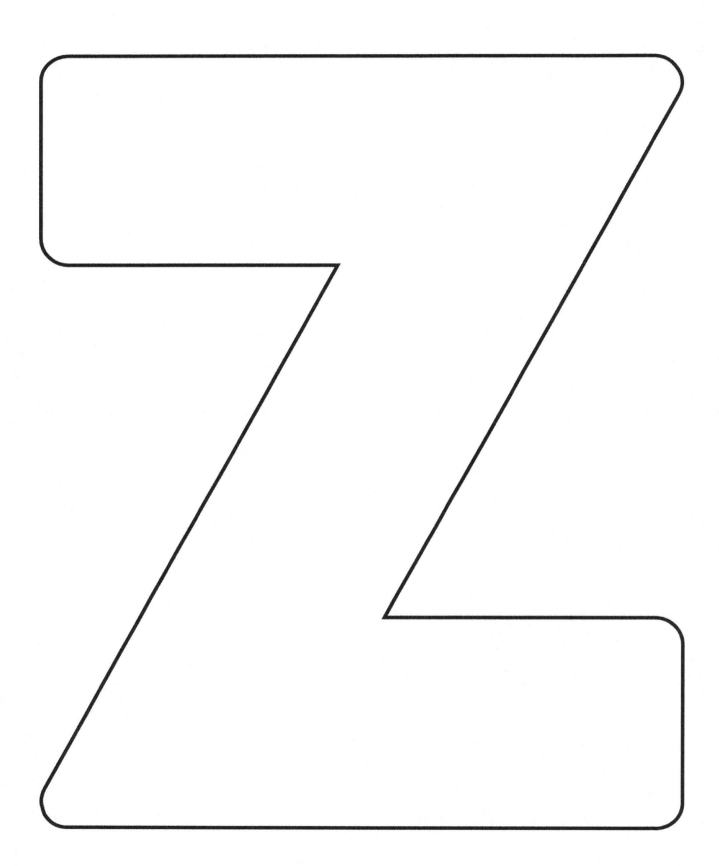

Congratulations

Certificate of
achievement

Awarded to

_____

for excellence in

Alphabet Coloring Book for Toddlers & Kids

Signed _____

Date _____

Made in the USA
Monee, IL
20 January 2021